VIGNETTES OF REVOLUTIONARY VIRGINIA

Vignettes of Revolutionary Virginia

REMARKABLE STORIES FROM THE FOUNDING OF THE NATION

Brent Tarter

RIVANNA BOOKS
UNIVERSITY OF VIRGINIA PRESS
Charlottesville and London

The University of Virginia Press is situated on the traditional lands of the Monacan Nation, and the Commonwealth of Virginia was and is home to many other Indigenous people. We pay our respect to all of them, past and present. We also honor the enslaved African and African American people who built the University of Virginia, and we recognize their descendants. We commit to fostering voices from these communities through our publications and to deepening our collective understanding of their histories and contributions.

RIVANNA BOOKS
An imprint of the University of Virginia Press

Printed in the United States of America on acid-free paper

First published 2026

1 3 5 7 9 8 6 4 2

LIBRARY OF CONGRESS CATALOGING-IN-PUBLICATION DATA
Names: Tarter, Brent, author
Title: Vignettes of revolutionary Virginia : remarkable stories from the founding of the nation / Brent Tarter.
Description: Charlottesville : Rivanna Books, University of Virginia Press, 2026. | Includes bibliographical references and index.
Identifiers: LCCN 2026003488 (print) | LCCN 2026003489 (ebook) | ISBN 9780813955384 hardback | ISBN 9780813955391 trade paperback | ISBN 9780813955407 ebook
Subjects: LCSH: Virginia—Social life and customs—18th century | Virginia—History—Revolution, 1775–1783 | Virginia—History—Colonial period, ca. 1600–1775 | Virginia—History—1775–1865
Classification: LCC F230 .T37 2026 (print) | LCC F230 (ebook)
LC record available at https://lccn.loc.gov/2026003488
LC ebook record available at https://lccn.loc.gov/2026003489

Cover art: "No Stamp Act" teapot, probably manufactured in Derby, England, 1765–ca. 1770s. (The Colonial Williamsburg Foundation; museum purchase)
Cover design: Cecilia Sorochin

CONTENTS

PREFACE

This is the second in a series of volumes of true stories about Virginians that I hope will interest readers and give easy access to some of the findings of the best modern historical scholarship. I began with *Vignettes of Colonial Virginia,* published in 2025. With *Vignettes of Revolutionary Virginia* I present brief accounts of episodes in the lives of several Virginians, some of whose names are not familiar, that illuminate how people lived and how their lives changed during and after the American Revolution. None of the people were representative Virginians, nor were they typical of most of their contemporaries. Instead, their personal experiences left behind a documentary record from which we can learn about some important events and the changes that took place in Virginia. I have adapted small portions of some of my previous publications for the purpose of placing these vignettes into the larger picture.

I could easily have selected other episodes from the lives of other Virginians for the same purpose or chosen to write about more of them or about fewer of them, but the events in the lives of these men and women are intrinsically interesting and revealing, and we know enough about the episodes and about the people and their times to place them into historical perspective and therefore understand them better. For the latter years of the eighteenth century, we are fortunate to have a considerable supply of surviving documents that contain the actual words of Virginia men and women. We can, as it were, listen to them. The documents help us understand how life for everyone in Virginia then was radically different from life for anyone in Virginia now. The episodes also illuminate the differences between the struggle for independence and the revolution that it set in motion and illustrate some of the consequences of the disconnect between the

Revolutionary language of liberty of 1776 and the continuing existence of slavery and of the hierarchical society of the colonial period.

Several of these episodes come directly from my own research into the original Virginia records of the period, especially during the eight years beginning in 1974 when I worked for the Virginia Independence Bicentennial Commission and had an office in a basement closet of the Virginia State Library (now the Library of Virginia). Under a plan that a statewide committee of white, male political leaders devised, we compiled and edited the records of the five colonial conventions and the many local committees that from 1774 to 1776 transformed Virginia from a royal colony into an independent commonwealth. As did many other scholars and most lay people in those days, we therefore paid much more attention to independence than to the revolution that independence let loose. We paid almost no attention to women, to Black Virginians free or enslaved, or to members of First Nations tribes. Indeed, we concentrated almost entirely on white, male political leaders and their actions.

As I hope that these vignettes demonstrate, historians now take a much longer and broader view, which is more inclusive and more thorough. Excellent research by a large number of men and women has enlarged the scope of our vision and caused us to revise our thinking on many subjects. We have even revised our thinking about the nature of politics and about the consequences of independence and the revolution, which in turn caused us to revise our overall interpretations of the period. Those revisions have persuaded me that for understanding how Virginians experienced the revolution and its consequences, we need to take a long view and begin when independence and revolution were unimaginable and conclude long after Americans had won their independence and adapted to many of the changes that the revolution caused.

A word or two about language. In these vignettes, the capitalized word *Black* does not refer to the skin color of people but to their social and cultural identifications with people of African birth or ancestry, whether free or enslaved. The most commonly used word to identify those people late in eighteenth-century Virginia was *colored,* which, along with *Negro, Afro-American,* and *African American,* is no more accurate as a physical description or cultural affiliation than *Black* and is subject to additional objections.

The capitalized term War for Independence often appears here in place of the more common Revolutionary War because it is important to distinguish the war from the revolution. In Virginia they were not the same thing, even though most people have conflated the two terms. The term "Revolutionary language of liberty" deserves to be foregrounded here, too, because of its importance in understanding the consequences for the future.

When I began to read about and research Virginia history fifty-several years ago, the subjects in the historical literature were almost all white, almost all male, overwhelmingly political, somewhat repetitious, and therefore often rather dull. The scholarship and popular histories exhibited a feeble attempt, by concentrating on a few admirable white men, to make inspiring a long narrative that exhibited a lack of change and that generally slighted or left out Black people, members of First Nations tribes, women of all races and classes, and most poor or otherwise ordinary white people. Important subjects like religion, economic change, social change, demographic change, material culture, women and gender relations, and other topics that directly affected the lives of the residents of Virginia got short shrift. Most appallingly, the subjects of slavery and racism got glossed over with apologetic language that almost literally whitewashed them and left behind a harmful residue of falsehood and misunderstanding. As I hope that these vignettes will demonstrate, the field of Virginia history and our understanding of Virginia history have changed dramatically.

I have had the almost unique opportunity to work in the original primary source documents of every decade of Virginia's history since the English invasion of 1607. I have also learned a great deal from a very large body of scholarship that excellent researchers published during my time as a Virginia historian. As a consequence of this published scholarship, historians no longer view Virginia history as we once did. My work in the original records has, I hope, enabled me to exploit what I found there to explain what nobody taught us when my generation was in school and what has been entirely too slow to get into the textbooks and popular literature that still shape how people understand their past.

We need to know about our shared past. The undoubtedly admirable portions of Virginia history cannot be understood properly without understanding the neglected portions or, most importantly, the unfortunate or even terrible portions of that past. Even as I have been writing, we still see people who are ignorant about that past or who have a narrow political agenda attempting to reshape the narrative of American history back into a celebration of elite white men and to deny or even prohibit students and curious readers from learning about and fully appreciating that all history is shared and that we all live in the aftermath of events that preceded us.

With *Vignettes of Revolutionary Virginia,* I hope to contribute to and continue to spread a more complete and accurate view of Virginia history outside the guild of professional historians. I said in April 2006 at the conclusion of my remarks at the opening session of the first Virginia Forum, the annual Virginia history conference, that "we have now an opportunity for the very first time to try to rewrite the history of all of Virginia and include the histories of all Virginians, including the Very First Families and African Americans, and not as add-ons or afterthoughts but as essential and integral dramatis personae. We need to try to make a history of Virginia that is a history that not only happened to everybody but a history that everybody made."

I published a revised and expanded version of that talk as "Making History in Virginia," *Virginia Magazine of History and Biography* 115 (2007): 2–55. My earlier needs-and-opportunities article that makes a similar point is "The New Virginia Bookshelf," *Virginia Magazine of History and Biography* 104 (1996): 7–102. I incorporated many of the new insights into my narrative history of Virginia, *Virginians and Their Histories* (Charlottesville: University of Virginia Press, 2020).

ACKNOWLEDGMENTS

I gladly thank all of my former colleagues at the Library of Virginia during the half-century that I researched and wrote about Virginia history there, especially the editors of the Library's *Dictionary of Virginia Biography* project, without which the lives of many Virginia men and women would remain almost entirely unknown, and the roles that they played, often unwittingly, in shaping the state in which we live would remain hidden from view. That work and other projects that I worked on at the Library of Virginia led me directly or indirectly to the stories of these people and to the documents that form the heart of these vignettes of life in revolutionary Virginia.

I also thank the many other historians, librarians, archivists, genealogists, local history researchers, and other people who published their discoveries about Virginia's history in the *Dictionary of Virginia Biography,* in the Virginia Humanities online *Encyclopedia Virginia,* in scholarly books, in articles in the scholarly literature, or as oral presentations at the annual state history conference, the Virginia Forum. Their work provided details and context and suggested how these episodes could inform us about aspects of Virginia's history in ways that the lives of the famous men and women whose stories populate our historical narratives often do not. That guild of scholars, like the Americans of whom Walt Whitman sang, contains multitudes, too many to list individually. The particular scholarship that some of those many researchers published and that illuminates these episodes in the lives of particular Virginians is listed in the suggestions for further reading at the end of the volume.

I also thank Mark Mones, acquisitions editor at the University of Virginia Press, who was enthusiastic about this project from the beginning; Lynne

Bonenberger, who copyedited the manuscript with her usual care, excellent suggestions, and good humor; Professor Woody Holton of the University of South Carolina and Professor Robert G. Parkinson of Binghamton University, both of whom read the manuscript for the Press, made useful suggestions, and endorsed publication; and Dale Neighbors and his colleagues in the Special Collections at the Library of Virginia for advice and assistance in selecting the illustrations.

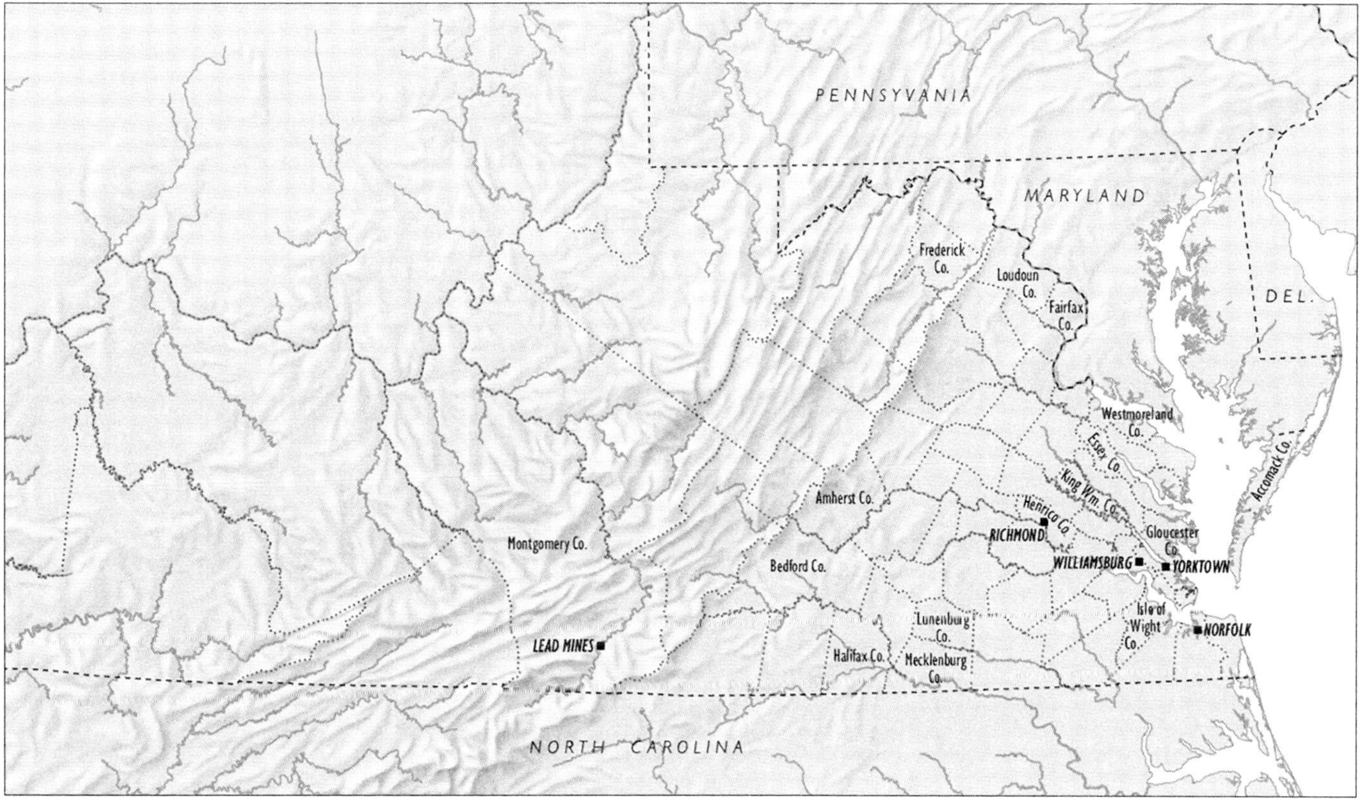

Virginia in 1780. (Map by Nat Case, INCase, LLC)

VIGNETTES OF REVOLUTIONARY VIRGINIA

1

An Unconstitutional Act of Parliament

On February 11, 1766, seven of the justices of the peace in Northampton County, Virginia, met in the regular monthly session of the county court. Northampton County is the southern of the two Virginia counties on the Eastern Shore, the peninsula between Chesapeake Bay and the Atlantic Ocean. The county clerk requested that the justices of the peace advise him and the residents of the county whether the Stamp Act that Parliament had passed in 1765 was binding on the inhabitants and whether the officials of the county would incur any penalties if they conducted their business without purchasing stamps as the act required. The seven justices of the peace "unanimously declared it to be their opinion that the said act did not bind, affect, or concern the inhabitants of this colony, inasmuch as they conceive the same to be unconstitutional." The clerk duly recorded the opinion on pages 31–32 of his official records, Northampton County Minute Book, 1765–71. He or one of the justices sent an attested copy to the printing office in Williamsburg, where Alexander Purdie and John Dixon printed it in the *Virginia Gazette* of March 21, 1766.

What was the Stamp Act? Why was it important? How did Virginians and other residents of the English colonies in North America react to it? And who gave the seven Eastern Shore men authority to declare that an act of Parliament was contrary to the constitution and that it consequently did not apply to the residents of their county or their entire colony?

George Grenville, King George III's first minister, announced in Parliament in 1764 that to help pay the huge public debt incurred during the Seven Years' (or French and Indian) War and to pay for stationing a large British armed force in North America to protect British interests in the colonies, Parliament would impose a stamp duty in the colonies the following year.

The General Assembly of Virginia petitioned the king in December 1764 not to sign the proposed law so as "to protect your People of this Colony in the Enjoyment of their ancient and inestimable Right of being governed by such Laws respecting their internal Polity and Taxation as are derived from their own Consent, with the Approbation of their Sovereign or his Substitute." The "Substitute" for the king was the royal governor or a lieutenant governor, who acted in the absence of a royal governor. The General Assembly, which consisted in part of elected members of the House of Burgesses, gave "Consent" on behalf of the burgesses' constituents to the bills that the legislature passed. No Virginian gave consent to any bills that Parliament passed.

The assembly defended its sole right to tax and legislate for Virginians as a "Right which as Men, and Descendents of *Britons,* they have ever quietly possessed since first by Royal Permission and Encouragement they left the Mother Kingdom to extend its Commerce and Dominion." The two Houses of the assembly also sent separate addresses to the two Houses of Parliament that it not pass the proposed bill and repeated their assertion that only elected Virginians could constitutionally tax Virginians.

The Stamp Act, which Parliament passed and King George III signed on March 22, 1765, required people to buy stamps from the government and affix them to legal documents, newspapers, playing cards, and numerous other important articles and services, much like the modern stamps on packets of cigarettes or on bottles of alcoholic beverages that signify payment of an excise tax. George Grenville also wanted to use it as a precedent that would permit Parliament to exercise a firmer control over the colonies of the expanding British empire.

People in nearly all of the North American colonies objected, chiefly because no Americans were represented in Parliament. Almost all American opponents of the Stamp Act declared that because it imposed a tax on residents of the colonies who had no part in electing members of the Parliament that passed it, the law violated the separate constitutional relationships that the people of each colony had with the king. Parliament had not had a role in developing the institutions and practices of colonial governments other than to regulate trans-Atlantic trade. Americans consequently believed that they and their own individual colonial legislatures had the same relationship to the king that the people and Parliament of Great Britain had, that each colony was a distinct and separate part of the king's realm and that therefore each colonial legislature was equal within its colony with Parliament in Great Britain.

The Northampton County justices of the peace may have gone further than anybody else in Virginia when in February 1766 they declared that the law was not in force in Virginia, but they were among the last public officials to make public their views about its unconstitutionality. In September 1765, the justices of the peace in Westmoreland County, southeast of Fredericksburg and across the bay from Northampton County, resigned rather than purchase the stamps or require residents of the county to purchase and use stamps as the law required. In October, justices of the peace in Stafford County, north of Fredericksburg, and in Culpeper County, west of Fredericksburg, all resigned, too. At a mass meeting in Westmoreland County less than three weeks after the action of that county's justices of the peace, 115 prominent local men signed a strong protest against the act.

By then, it would have been very difficult for anybody in Virginia to purchase stamps or paper with stamps printed on it. When the stamps and the stamp distributor arrived in Williamsburg in October 1765, a large and angry crowd of men forced him to resign and to load the stamps back aboard the ship that had transported him to Virginia.

Several of the colonies had sent representatives to the Stamp Act Congress in New York late in 1765, but Virginia was not represented in the congress. In May of that year, Patrick Henry had spoken out so strongly in the House of Burgesses against the Stamp Act that he incurred charges of speaking treasonous words because he appeared to criticize the king for signing the act. The lieutenant governor, acting in place of the absentee royal governor, dissolved the assembly, which terminated the session. The legislators did not meet again until late in 1766, so the assembly was not in session to elect Virginia delegates to the Stamp Act Congress, which opponents of the act in other colonies called after the end of the assembly session.

The separate actions of Virginians were nevertheless very influential. Newspapers up and down the east coast printed Patrick Henry's draft resolutions, some of which the House of Burgesses adopted, some of which it did not adopt, and some of which it adopted but almost immediately repealed. Henry's resolutions sparked spirited debate and continued controversy. In the spring of 1766, Virginian Richard Bland published a treatise, *Inquiry into the Rights of the British Colonies.* He was a leading member of the House of Burgesses, a distinguished General Court lawyer, and the most knowledgeable student of Virginia's history and laws. He argued that "the civil Constitution of *England*" did not fix "the proper Connexion between the Colonies and the Mother Kingdom" or define "what their reciprocal Duties to each other are, and what Obedience is due from the Children to the Parent."

From the colonial constitution as it had evolved, Bland defined the nature of the relationship between the king and his Virginia subjects. Bland concluded that Parliament (king, lords, and commons all acting together) had no constitutional authority to legislate for or to impose taxes on Virginians for any other purpose than to defend the empire and regulate trans-Atlantic trade. The colonists' political connections with Great Britain were exclusively as subjects of the king.

Bland did not then state new propositions. Instead, he compiled systematic legal and historical arguments from precedents and from the historical record to explain the proper relationship of the people of Virginia to the king and Parliament, an argument that was widely understood and accepted in North America at that time. It was a version of the origins of all government, of the social contract, except that it was not rooted in antiquity when people sought safety under the dominion of a warlord, chief, or king to whom they pledged allegiance. It had its origins in the relatively recent past of colonists who had created colonial governments under the authority of and with the permission and participation of their king. Bland concluded, as many other Americans concluded, that their political tie with Great Britain was as subjects of the king and that they owed no obedience to Parliament.

It is impossible to know precisely what proportion of the white residents of the North American colonies opposed the Stamp Act. Some men published pamphlets or articles in newspapers to attempt to persuade Americans to submit peacefully to the authority of the king and Parliament. We know that opposition was clearly widespread, though. Many colonists supported putting pressure on British merchants to persuade Parliament to repeal the Stamp Act. One ingenious English entrepreneur capitalized on the opposition. He manufactured teapots for the American market decorated with a "No Stamp Act" label. Tea was a very popular drink in North America

One English manufacturer produced and sold this teapot to colonial Americans during the Stamp Act crisis. (The Colonial Williamsburg Foundation; museum purchase)

at the time, but it is a curious irony that a form of protest against the act of Parliament was a teapot; less than a decade later, it was an act of Parliament to tax colonial purchases of tea that drove the colonies together into a new league in opposition to Parliament's actions and assertions of authority.

The combined arguments and economic pressure of the colonists persuaded the king's new ministers to yield in 1766, and they pushed through Parliament a bill to repeal the Stamp Act. At the same time, though, Parliament passed and the king signed An Act for the Better Securing the Dependency of His Majesty's Dominions in America upon the Crown and Parliament of Great Britain. The Declaratory Act, as it was commonly known, stated flatly that Parliament "had, hath, and of right ought to have, full power and authority to make laws and statutes of sufficient force and validity to bind the colonies and people of America, subjects of the Crown of Great Britain, in all cases whatsoever."

The Declaratory Act made official what the authors of the Stamp Act intended to do: provide a precedent for Parliament to crack down on colonial governments that acted in ways that the king's ministers, who were all members of Parliament, disliked. In the general rejoicing in the colonies at the repeal of the Stamp Act, most people initially failed to appreciate the full implications of the Declaratory Act. Parliament claimed unlimited authority to tax and to legislate for the colonies, a much more expansive power than the colonists had objected to in the particular instance of the Stamp Act.

It should be noted here that until 1776, Americans did not directly criticize the actions of the king. To implicate the king in jeopardizing the liberties of Americans was virtually treason. Instead, the protestors blamed the king's ministers (members of his cabinet), who were also members of Parliament and who managed the executive offices of the royal government in the name of the king.

Beginning with the 1764 announcement that Parliament would impose a stamp tax on the colonists, a new controversy concerning the power of Parliament to tax or regulate colonial activities—which is to say, a new controversy that threatened the independent status of colonial legislatures and the rights of colonists—arose every year or two until Americans declared their independence of the king. By then, relations had significantly soured, and the Boston Tea Party of December 1773 and Parliament's enactment of what the British called the Coercive Acts and the colonists called the Intolerable Acts precipitated the assembling of the First Continental Congress in September 1774.

Just before the First Virginia Convention, the first of five, met in August 1774 to elect delegates to represent the colony in Congress, Thomas Jefferson published *A Summary View of the Rights of British America.* Jefferson made essentially the same argument that Bland had made, but Jefferson found the origins of English, and therefore of American, liberty further back in time than Bland did, in a somewhat mythic Saxon past. Jefferson's *Summary View* characterized the crises of the 1760s and 1770s as a resumption of centuries of royal encroachments on and destructions of historic Saxon liberty. That implicated the king, not merely Parliament, in a more scholarly way and with marginally less bluntness than Patrick Henry's Stamp Act resolutions and speech of 1765.

In the decade between the Stamp Act and the calling of the First Continental Congress, Americans debated the implications of the opposition that a large number of them believed that they were justified in making to the actions of Parliament. To opponents, those acts appeared to restrict the widely accepted, constitutional authority of the colonial legislatures and threaten the essential liberties of residents of the colonies. During that decade, the arguments did not significantly change, but the circumstances and the potential consequences of colonial opposition to the British escalated in intensity.

The action of the Northampton County justices of the peace in February 1766 when they declared that the Stamp Act did not apply in Virginia was bolder than the actions of the justices of the peace in the three other counties, who merely resigned, or the other Americans who only complained that the law was unjust or unconstitutional. The seven men in Northumberland County asserted that they had authority to exercise a right that no subject of the king of Great Britain anywhere possessed, to declare an act of Parliament inoperative. Only Parliament—king, House of Lords, and House of Commons—could change the British Constitution, which was becoming, in effect, an emerging imperial constitution, and they did so in the Declaratory Act when they claimed full authority to tax and pass new laws that governed Virginians and all other Americans. The Northampton County justices of the peace objected to Parliament's attempt to change the colonial constitutions and the relationship of the residents of the colonies with the king.

Two questions: Who were the justices of the peace, and who gave them authority to declare that an act of Parliament was unconstitutional and did not apply in Virginia?

First: In each county, one or two dozen men served as justices of the peace under the authority of a commission that the royal governor or lieutenant governor issued in the name of the king. Many of the justices of the peace had no training in the law but served because they were among the most prosperous and respectable men in their counties. Individually, they had authority to authenticate documents, issue arrest warrants in some cases, and execute any of a number of other administrative responsibilities. Sitting together, they served as judges of the county court, which exercised a wide array of legislative, executive, and judicial responsibilities in the county. The courts recommended men to the governor for appointment as sheriff or constable and to fill vacancies on the bench, so that the county courts had become unelected, undemocratic little local oligarchies.

Second: Nobody gave the justices of the peace authority to declare that an act of Parliament was unconstitutional. They merely asserted that it was. Twenty-first-century Americans are accustomed to a legal system in which courts of law make final determinations whether legislative or executive actions violate the national constitution or the constitution of a state, but nobody had that authority in the eighteenth century, which is perhaps one reason why the disputes about Parliamentary authority dragged on without resolution for more than a decade before independence. Judicial review, as the legal process of courts making final determinations on questions of constitutionality is known, did not become firmly established in American jurisprudence until after the Supreme Court of the United States first exercised it in *Marbury v. Madison* in 1803. The author of the ruling in that case, Chief Justice John Marshall, of Virginia, might have, but did not, cite the long-forgotten ruling of the Northampton County Court in 1766 as a possible precedent.

2

What Is It We Are Contending Against?

ON JULY 20, 1774, George Washington wrote a long letter to an old friend, Brian Fairfax. It had been ten years since the first announcement of the Stamp Act, nine years since Parliament passed it, and eight years since Parliament repealed it and passed the Declaratory Act. It also was one year before Congress appointed Washington to be commanding general of the Continental Army, and two years before Congress declared independence. As the letter indicates, in the spring and summer of 1774, political affairs in the colonies took a very serious turn.

Washington's letter is one of the best summaries of the position that American colonists had been taking in their prolonged conflict with the British government about the claim of Parliament to tax residents of the colonies and to legislate for them, as the Declaratory Act of 1766 stated it, "in all cases whatsoever." The letter also demonstrates that Washington perfectly understood the implications of what the colonists had already done and that they had to protect their liberties with measures strong enough to counter the threat. The original letter, in Washington's clear, distinctive handwriting, is in the Virginia Historical Society (now the Virginia Museum of History and Culture) and was published in W. W. Abbot et al., eds., *Papers of George Washington, Colonial Series,* 10 vols. (Charlottesville, 1983–95), 10:109–10.

The reputation of Washington as a thinker and writer has not stood up very well beside such multitalented founders as James Madison, Thomas Jefferson, Alexander Hamilton, Benjamin Franklin, and John Adams. Few men or women of any generation could stand on the same intellectual level with those five. Unlike them (Franklin excepted), Washington did not have a proper, classical education. He did not study, read, or speak Latin or Greek,

George Washington (1732–99) in the uniform of a colonel of the Virginia militia, by Charles Willson Peale, 1772. (The Museums of Washington and Lee University)

nor did he speak or read French, the ancient and modern languages that educated and cultured English and Virginia gentlemen of the eighteenth century believed that they should know.

Uneducated by classical standards, Washington was nevertheless a careful reader and close student of politics and world affairs, as well as of the emerging field of scientific agriculture. He had spent his early life as a land surveyor, which required him to make precise measurements, close observations, and careful calculations. It is evident from the letter that Washington had made careful calculations about the implications for American colonists of what Parliament had done and what the colonists might have to do in the future to protect themselves and their colonial constitutions from Parliament.

Washington was also a clear, persuasive, and occasionally eloquent writer. Like many of his contemporaries, he had his own ideas about spelling, punctuation, abbreviations, and capitalization. He also wrote some very long run-on sentences. It can help to read some of them aloud. Washington's letter to Brian Fairfax is an excellent example of George Washington at his best before the burdens of military command fell on his shoulders in June 1775, when the Continental Congress appointed him commander in chief of the Continental Army.

The occasion for Washington to write his letter to Fairfax in July 1774 was a difference of opinion that they had about very recent political events in Virginia. Almost every year since 1764, when George Grenville announced his intention to impose a stamp tax on Americans, a new political controversy erupted that renewed discussions and debates about the rights of colonial Americans and the authority of Parliament. In hindsight, it looks as if the events followed one another in quick succession, and that Americans were constantly preoccupied with the subject. In fact, discussions continued off and on for almost a full decade, like a recurring political toothache or a series of attacks of gout.

Washington was a member of the House of Burgesses during the session that began in May 1774, five months after the Boston Tea Party, in which men dumped into Boston harbor more than two hundred chests of tea that altogether probably weighed several thousand pounds. The East India Company had shipped the tea to Boston, but the Tea Party prevented customs officials from landing the tea and making it subject to a tax that Parliament placed on imported tea. News arrived during the session of the Virginia General Assembly that Parliament had passed the first of several Coercive Acts to punish the city of Boston and the colony of Massachusetts and to strengthen British control over the protesting colonists. One of the Coercive Acts, the Massachusetts Government Act, dissolved the royal charter of the colony, whereupon the king appointed General Thomas Gage military governor of Massachusetts. Most Americans eventually called the collection of Coercive Acts the Intolerable Acts, which clearly expressed their opinion about the acts of Parliament.

The House of Burgesses adopted strong resolutions that condemned the first of the Coercive Acts, which closed the port of Boston to all commerce until the people of the city reimbursed the East India Company for the destroyed tea. After the royal governor dissolved the assembly, which terminated the session, the Virginia Committee of Correspondence received news of the passage of the remainder of the Coercive Acts and joined with the Committee of Correspondence in Massachusetts to call together the First Continental Congress.

In order to select the Virginia delegates to the Congress, the burgesses who remained in Williamsburg after the termination of the assembly session, including George Washington, issued a call for a convention to meet in Williamsburg in August. Many Virginians believed that the action was unwise or even dangerous. Washington wrote to Brian Fairfax to explain why he joined in without hesitation.

"That I differ very widely from you," Washington began, "in respect to the mode of obtaining a repeal of the Acts so much, & so justly complaind of, I shall not hesitate to acknowledge; & that this difference in opinion may, probably, proceed from the different Construction's"—understandings, or explanations—"we put upon the Conduct, & Intention of the Ministry, may also be true; But as I see nothing on the one hand, to induce a belief that the Parliament would embrace a favourable oppertunity of Repealing Acts which they go on with great rapidity to pass, in order to enforce their Tyrannical System; and on the other, observe, or think I observe, that Government is pursuing a regular Plan at the expence of Law & justice, to overthrow our Constitutional Rights & liberties, how can I expect any redress from a Measure which hath been ineffectually tryd already—" The long dash at the end of a sentence acted like a period, or full stop, in the eighteenth century.

"For Sir," Washington continued, "what is it we are contending against? Is it against paying the duty of 3d. pr lb."—three pennies per pound—"on Tea because burthensome? No, it is the Right only, we have all along disputed." That is, the right that Parliament claimed to tax Americans, which Americans believed only their own colonial legislatures, which included elected members, could legitimately do. Washington recalled that "to this end we have already Petitiond his Majesty in as humble, & dutiful a manner as Subjects could do; nay more, we applied to the House of Lords, & House of Commons in their different Legislative Capacities setting forth that, as Englishmen, we could not be deprivd of this essential, & valuable part of our Constitution, If then (as the Fact really is) it is against the Right of Taxation, we now do, & (as I before said) all along have contended, why should they suppose an exertion of this power would be less obnoxious now, than formerly? and what reasons have we to believe that, they would make a Second attempt whilst the same Sentiments fill'd the Breast of every American, if they did not intend to inforce it if possible?"

In effect replying to objections that the men who were responsible for the Boston Tea Party had been guilty of riotously destroying private property, Washington pointed out the injustice of Parliament's punishing the entire population of the city by cutting off its trade, rather than punishing the men who took part. "The conduct of the Boston People could not justify the rigour of their Measures, unless their had been a requisition of payment & refusal of it; nor did that measure require an Act to deprive the Governmt of Massachusets Bay of their Charter; or to exempt Offenders from tryal in the place, where Offences were Committed, as there was not, nor could not be, a single Instance produced to manifest the necessity of it—"

Washington drew what he believed were the unavoidable lessons from the conduct of Parliament and the king's ministers. "Are not all these things self evident proofs of a fixed & uniform Plan to Tax us? If we want further proofs, does not all the Debates in the House of Commons serve to confirm this? and hath not Genl Gage's Conduct"—Thomas Gage was the new military governor of Massachusetts, whom the Massachusetts Government Act authorized the king to appoint—"since his arrival (in Stopping the Address of his Council, & Publishing a Proclamation more becoming a Turkish Bashaw than an English Govr & declaring it Treason to associate in any manner by which the Commerce of Great Britain is to be affected) exhibited unexampled Testimony of the most despotick System of Tyranny that ever was practiced in a free Government."

"In short," Washington concluded, "what further proofs are wanting to satisfy one of the design's of the Ministry than their own Acts; which are uniform, & plainly tending to the same point—nay, if I mistake not, avowedly to fix the Right of Taxation—what hope then from Petitioning, when they tell us that now, or never, is the time to fix the matter—shall we after this whine & cry for releif, when we have already tried it in vain?, or shall we supinely sit, and see one Provence after another fall a Sacrafice to Despotism? If I was in any doubt as to the Right wch the Parliament of Great Britain had to Tax us without our Consents, I should most heartily coincide with you in opinion, that to Petition, & petition only, is the proper method to apply for relief; because we should then be asking a favour, & not claiming a Right wch by the Law of Nature & our Constitution we are, in my opinion, indubitably entitled to; I should even think it criminal to go further than this, under such an Idea; but none such I have."

Washington selected an apt figure of speech to conclude his letter to Fairfax. "I think the Parliament of Great Britain hath no more Right to put their hands into my Pocket, without my consent, than I have to put my hands into you'rs, for money, and this being already urged to them in a firm, but decent manner by all the Colonies, what reason is there to expect any thing from their justice?"

Between the beginning of June 1774, when the burgesses called the First Virginia Convention, and August, when the convention met, hundreds of white men, most of them undoubtedly voters, in many or most Virginia counties endorsed the participation of their burgesses in the forthcoming convention or adopted instructions to the men who planned to attend. Resolutions adopted in twenty-nine of Virginia's sixty-one counties appeared in the colony's newspapers, and it is quite likely that resolutions that men adopted in other counties have since disappeared because they were not then printed. George Washington and his friend and neighbor George Mason apparently prepared the resolutions that voters in their county of Fairfax adopted. Perhaps because of the fame of the authors, the Fairfax County resolutions became the most well known. They were, indeed, more thoughtful and better written than some, but they did not differ from the others in substance. In a remarkable display of unity of purpose among the local political leaders throughout Virginia, all of the surviving resolutions and instructions opposed Parliament's claim of legitimate authority to tax or legislate for the colonies.

In August 1774, Washington returned to Williamsburg to attend the First Virginia Convention, which elected him to the seven-member delegation it named to represent Virginia in the First Continental Congress. The convention also adopted what it called an association to prohibit the importation or sale of a long list of British merchandise and specifically including tea. The purpose of the boycott was to pressure British merchants to persuade Parliament to change its policy, a tactic that had worked in 1765–66 when colonial pressure persuaded Parliament to repeal the Stamp Act of 1765.

Many or most of Washington's contemporary Americans, although they opposed the encroachments that Parliament and the king's ministers had made on colonial rights, were reluctant to pursue measures that could lead to actual conflict. Washington, on the other hand, was among the first few who had the foresight to appreciate that one clear consequence of continued strong resistance to an increasingly serious threat could be armed conflict, and he thought that it was necessary to be bold enough to recognize that fact and act accordingly.

A South Carolina man on his way to represent that colony in the First Continental Congress in Philadelphia heard a story as he passed through Virginia that August. Whether the story was true is impossible to prove. The man told John Adams, of Massachusetts, what he had heard, and Adams recorded it in his diary at the end of the month. Adams wrote that Washington had declared in a speech to the Virginia Convention at the beginning of the month, "I will raise 1000 Men, subsist them at my own Expence"—pay them and all of their expenses—"and march my self at their Head for the Relief of Boston."

3

The Alternative of Williamsburg

THE FIRST CONTINENTAL CONGRESS met in Philadelphia from September 5 through October 26, 1774, with Peyton Randolph, Speaker of the House of Burgesses of Virginia, as president. On October 20, the members adopted the Continental Association, which resembled the association that Virginians had adopted at the First Virginia Convention in August to refuse to import or purchase any of several items of British merchandise until Parliament ceased taxing Americans. That tactic had worked in 1765 and 1766 when Americans insisted on the repeal of the Stamp Act, and they thought that it would work again.

Peyton Randolph and two other Virginia delegates left Philadelphia soon after Congress adopted the association and before the adjournment to return to Williamsburg for the anticipated meeting of the General Assembly that the governor had called for November 3. The three men arrived on October 30 and had the Continental Association printed in the next issues of the Williamsburg newspapers. The General Assembly did not meet, however. What one of the newspapers described as "a considerable Number" of burgesses assembled in the Capitol, but the governor was not present because he had raised volunteers and marched into the upper Ohio Valley to confront the Shawnee and bring to an end a series of low-intensity conflicts between them and western Virginians.

While the burgesses were still in Williamsburg, a very large number of the colony's merchants assembled for their regular twice-a-year meeting. Reports of how many burgesses and merchants were present vary widely, ranging up to four or five hundred. In public meetings between November 4 and 7, with Peyton Randolph presiding, burgesses, merchants, and bystanders signed the Continental Association.

Henry Fleming was there and described some of what happened in a letter to his employers. Fleming was an Englishman who resided in Virginia and worked to collect money that Virginians owed to an English mercantile firm. His letter is dated November 1, 1774, but he did not conclude it until later, which we know because he described events in Williamsburg that happened after that date. The original, recipients' copy of the letter apparently does not survive, but Fleming copied it or prepared the first draft in his letter book, a bound volume of the sort in which merchants, public officials, and other people who regularly wrote or received correspondence kept copies of their outgoing letters. Fleming's copy is in the Letter Book of Henry Fleming, 1772–1775, Papers of Henry Fleming, 1772–1795, Cumbria Record Office, Carlisle, United Kingdom.

As with some other letters from seventeenth- and eighteenth-century residents of Virginia, it can help to read the passage aloud and let the rhythms of the human voice smooth out the tangled syntax. "America it's said is contending for *Liberty!*" Fleming complained to his employers, "at same time they deny the British Merchts resident here the liberty of pursuing their interest in a legal manner, of speaking their opinions, & almost of thinking contrary to *their* opinions.—There was a Pole erected upon the parade in Wmburg when I was there with a Brush a Bag of Feathers & a Tar Barrel at its foot by order of the Burgesses to intimidate such as would dare to broach a sentiment contrary to what is calld the liberties of America. Hanging Drowning Ducking, Taring & Feathering, Beating to death & Gouging was threatend. & recommended in my hearing." Fleming concluded, "In short whilst some are contending for Liberty they are willing to deprive others of every pretention to it from which I conclude every one here is a Tyrant as far as his power extends."

An engraving of the scene, executed later in England and based on eyewitness descriptions such as Fleming's, bore the title *The Alternative of Williams-Burg*. It depicts the Virginians in a decidedly and deliberately unflattering manner. Some people have speculated that the engraving represented the scene in Williamsburg in August 1774 when the First Virginia Convention adopted the Virginia Association, but there are no contemporary references

The Alternative of Williams-Burg, a London engraver's unflattering 1775 depiction of Virginia patriots forcing merchants to sign the Continental Association in November 1774. (Library of Congress, Prints & Photographs Division)

to any such events at that time. Letters from men who were present for the November joint meeting of burgesses and merchants, including Fleming, described the scene in detail and indicated that the meeting inspired the image. Under the circumstances, the events in Williamsburg were undoubtedly very troubling, perhaps even frightening.

The association of merchants faced its own problems. The Virginia and Continental Associations prohibited importations of numerous articles of merchandise from Britain. That, together with the expiration of an essential Virginia statute, had brought commerce almost to a standstill. In May 1774, when the burgesses passed resolutions to condemn the Boston Port Bill, the royal governor abruptly dissolved the General Assembly, which put an end to its work. The legislators had not yet renewed the law that regulated the fees that county officials charged for conducting business in the county courts. As a result, debt collection suits in many county courts stalled. Fleming and some other people at the time referred to that with exaggeration as an actual closing of the courts. The absence of the governor and of several General Court lawyers who were serving in Congress may have meant that the General Court could not handle any of the debt suits that were on its docket, either, for want of a quorum. That was what Fleming referred to when he wrote that Virginians had denied "British Merchts resident here the liberty of pursuing their interest in a legal manner." Some of the merchants complained that scarcely a shilling changed hands at the meeting in Williamsburg.

The experience of Henry Fleming was not unique, and episodes of threatening and even violence were not restricted to the vicinity of Williamsburg. One unfortunate consequence of the organized crowds—mobs—of people who gathered to intimidate their political opponents was that citizens who described themselves as champions of American liberties denied other men and women their basic rights to express their opinions—as we shall see.

4

The Yorktown Tea Party

THE BOSTON TEA PARTY that took place in December 1773 marks, in many people's minds, the beginning of the struggle for independence and the American Revolution. That is perhaps debatable, inasmuch as Americans had by then been objecting to and organizing protests against British policies for almost a decade. The Tea Party was certainly a major escalation of tactics. What is not debatable, even though it is not very well known except to a few historians who specialize in the period, is that the Boston Tea Party was not the only such event involving imported tea. Similar tea parties took place in several other colonies, including one in Yorktown, Virginia.

The Virginia Association that members of the First Virginia Convention put into effect in August 1774 and the Continental Association that the First Continental Congress adopted in October of that year prohibited the importation of numerous items of British merchandise and specifically prohibited the importation, sale, and consumption of tea. The two associations also authorized men in every county and town to form a committee, in the words of the Continental Association, "to observe the conduct of all persons touching this association" and to make public the results of its inquiries into charges that people had violated its terms, "to the end that all such foes to the rights of British-America may be publickly known, and universally contemned as the enemies of American liberty." The local committees were always called county or city committees, but in the twentieth century when some of the records of the committees were first published, they received the incorrect title of committees of safety.

Early in November 1774, the ship *Virginia* arrived at Yorktown carrying, among many other things, two half-chests of tea that John Norton and

Sons, a London shipping firm that conducted a large and profitable trade with Virginia tobacco planters, had sent to Williamsburg shopkeeper John Prentis. On November 7, several residents of Yorktown asked for advice from some of the prominent men in Williamsburg about how to proceed with respect to the tea. (This was the very week of the scene in Williamsburg that Henry Fleming described.) The men of Yorktown boarded the *Virginia* and waited a short time for advice from Williamsburg, but hearing nothing, they "hoisted the Tea out of the Hold and threw it into the River, and then returned to the Shore," according to a newspaper report of the event, "without doing Damage to the Ship or any other Part of her Cargo."

Across the York River in Gloucester County, members of the newly elected Gloucester County Committee met that morning to learn what the burgesses in Williamsburg advised the men in Yorktown to do; but in the afternoon, when they had still received no news, they crossed the river and also boarded the *Virginia*. They learned that the "Tea had met with its deserved Fate, for it had been committed to the Waves."

The members of the Gloucester County Committee returned home, reported to other members of the committee, and resumed their meeting, at which they adopted several resolutions. One condemned Prentis, "who wrote for and to whom the Tea was consigned," because he had "justly incurred the Censure of this Country, and that he ought to be made a publick Example of." The committee also declared that Captain Howard Esten, for allowing the tea to be carried aboard his ship, "has acted imprudently, by which he has drawn on himself the Displeasure of the People of this County." The committee ordered that the *Virginia* depart within twenty days and return to London and that no resident of the county send any tobacco to England aboard the ship.

The Gloucester County Committee rebuked the senior partner of the shipping firm in strong words: "John Norton, Merchant in London, by sending over Tea in his Ship, has lent his *little Aid* to the Ministry for enslaving America, and been guilty of a daring Insult upon the People of this Colony, to whom he owes his ALL." The committee adopted a second resolution declaring that "the said Norton has forfeited all Title to the Confidence of this County, and that we will not in future consign Tobacco, or any other Commodity, to his House, until satisfactory Concessions are made; and we recommend the same Resolution to the rest of the Colony."

That was not the end. On January 5, 1775, John Norton, on behalf of his firm, addressed a letter to the inhabitants of Virginia. He explained that because the company had received information about the Virginia Association that was adopted in August 1774 (or an earlier, less formal association that some men created in May of that year), the company officers had been uneasy about shipping the tea that Prentis had ordered. They detained the *Virginia* in London for two weeks past its planned sailing date. Finally, "much against their inclinations," the company's officers complied with Prentis's request, but they gave Captain Esten instructions to consult members of the relevant committee as soon as he arrived and to comply with the committee's recommendations or requirements. The letter, which was published on May 6, 1775, in one of the several newspapers titled the *Virginia Gazette,* concluded with a hope that "the imputation of injustice to America will cease, that truth will trample over calumny by misrepresentation, and that they"—officers and employees of John Norton and Sons—"shall recover that place which they formerly held in the esteem of their friends and countrymen in Virginia."

John Norton had lived in Yorktown for two decades or more as a junior partner in the English tobacco trading firm of Flowerdewe and Norton. After he returned to England, he formed his own company, John Norton and Sons. One of those sons, John Hatley Norton, resided in Yorktown at the time of the tea party and was married to a daughter of the treasurer of the colony. The firm had friends as well as countrymen in Virginia. It was to the advantage of the two Nortons as well as their business associates to do what they could to cultivate good relationships with residents of Virginia, including members of the committees, who were all local dignitaries and men of influence.

Encounters between merchants and shippers, between merchants and tobacco planters, and between committee members and other Virginians produced an unknown but undoubtedly large number of episodes throughout the colony that created suspicions or animosities in communities. Delays of weeks or months in transportation of letters and news items across the Atlantic Ocean no doubt frustrated people and made matters worse. In this instance, Captain Esten made a fast crossing to Yorktown and undoubtedly made another fast return to London after the Yorktown

Tea Party, which enabled John Norton to write his reply to the Gloucester County Committee in January. Norton's letter, however, did not make a fast crossing back to Virginia and was not published until May, six months after the Yorktown Tea Party. By then, the political temperature in Virginia had drastically risen, and the Yorktown Tea Party was probably a dim memory.

5

John Hook, of Bedford County

DURING THE WINTER OF 1774–75, men formed county and town committees almost everywhere in Virginia. The committees usually consisted of one or two dozen locally notable men, but the number varied rather widely. For the most part, committee members were local justices of the peace, vestrymen of their parishes of the Church of England, or members of leading planter families, the traditional political leaders in every county and town. In some instances, however, new men who were not already part of the governing elite won election in counties with a larger number of committee members.

The elected committees were an innovation in Virginia. Until that time, the only elected public officials in the colony were members of the House of Burgesses, with one occasional exception: every few years, the General Assembly dissolved a dysfunctional vestry of one of the Virginia parishes of the Church of England and authorized voters to elect new vestrymen. The committee system represented the first widespread election of men to manage local affairs in Virginia, and in that sense was a small democratic reform. It is true that some men formed local committees earlier to enforce an embargo on British goods after Parliament levied new taxes on the colonists, but surviving records do not indicate that those committees were numerous, active, or long-lasting.

As with the proceedings of the Gloucester County Committee concerning the importation of tea aboard the *Virginia* in the autumn of 1774, the committees vigilantly oversaw commerce in the countryside as well as in the several Virginia ports and also investigated charges that local men opposed the associations, even if they had not violated them. Surviving county committee records exist in whole or in part for a large majority of the counties and have been collected and published, along with convention journals and other records, in volumes 2 through 7 of William J. Van Schreeven, Robert L. Scribner, and Brent Tarter, eds., *Revolutionary Virginia, The Road to Independence: A Documentary Record,* 7 vols. (Charlottesville, 1973–83).

In May 1775, John Hook came under suspicion by members of the Bedford County Committee. We know about the event not because records of the committee survive, but because a summons that the committee issued to Hook and his reply are preserved in the John Hook Papers, Duke University, along with other correspondence and records of the country stores that Hook ran for several decades. The summons and Hook's reply are printed in *Revolutionary Virginia, The Road to Independence,* 3:230, 234–35.

Bedford County is in the foothills of the Blue Ridge Mountains near Lynchburg, where John Lynch operated a ferry across the James River. The town was named for him, but the most prominent local resident was his brother, Charles Lynch, a burgess and colonel in the county militia and almost certainly the man whose surname later became associated with illegal mob punishments or killings of people. At a muster of volunteer Bedford County militiamen in May 1775, Hook talked with Charles Lynch about the political ferment in the colonies and very likely about the resolution that the Second Virginia Convention had adopted in March to put the colony into a state of defense and to arm volunteers to re-create the militia that the expiration of the colony's militia law in May 1774 had effectively dissolved. Patrick Henry had introduced the resolution and made his now famous Liberty of Death speech in support of its adoption.

At the militia muster, Hook and Lynch discussed a report that some volunteers in neighboring Botetourt County had objected to the possibility of being sent out of Virginia to help defend the people of another colony and leaving the residents of their own county in potential danger. According to the charge in the committee's summons to Hook to appear at the next committee meeting and explain his conduct, Hook had told Lynch, "in the warmest manner, & swore by God, there never will be peace till the Americans get well Floged." Lynch reported the conversation to the committee and accused Hook of being "an unworthy member of Society." Lynch also informed the committee that Hook had dispersed "a number of Pamphlets wrote against the American cause with an intention of raising divitions among the People." The surviving records do not identify the pamphlets.

A brief record of an action of the Bedford County Committee on June 27 appeared in one of the two *Virginia Gazettes* published in Williamsburg, but that notice does not contain a reference to John Hook. In Hook's papers, however, is a draft letter to the committee in Hook's handwriting. The committee may have considered it at the June 27 meeting or at some other meeting for which no record survives. In the letter, Hook explained that when he referred to Americans being well flogged, he meant only the men in Boston who had destroyed East India Company tea in December 1773. He also explained that he had distributed pamphlets to various people but did not discuss the contents of them with any but a few friends. "I assure this Committee," Hook wrote, "that I had no kind of design in bringing those Pamphlets to this County, more then to inform my Self both sides of the question."

One of the interesting and sometimes overlooked things that happened in Virginia during the years of protests against British policies was that newspapers and pamphlets were handed about, read, and discussed in places where there was no local printing press or where people may have seldom even seen newspapers. Nearly all of the newspapers published in the American colonies at that time were weekly publications printed in coastal towns and cities. Virginia had two weekly newspapers published in Williamsburg, both entitled the *Virginia Gazette,* and one published in Norfolk that also had that name and an explanatory subtitle, *Virginia Gazette, or the Norfolk Intelligencer.* Judging by the amount of Virginia news and the number of advertisements that appear in some of the weekly newspapers published in Annapolis and in Philadelphia, those newspapers may have been more common in some parts of northern and northeastern Virginia than the Williamsburg papers. In any event, news about the political turmoil and newspaper articles and pamphlets that expressed various opinions got handed about and discussed very widely, even in John Hook's Bedford County, 200 miles from the nearest printing office.

Hook concluded his letter to the county committee with a promise to keep quiet about his political opinions because they were clearly different from those of a large number, perhaps a majority, of his neighbors; "and as to the Pamphlets I will deliver them up to the Committee to be delt with as they please." The final part of Hook's promise resembled the almost humble remarks of other men who did not fully approve of the radical steps that their neighbors and committee members heartily endorsed. "When I Assure this Committee that I wish the Liberty and Prosperity of this Countrey as sincerely as any of them possibly can do I hope a difference in oppinion as to the mode of Attaining the same, will not be judged sufficient grounds for declaring one of such Sentiments an enemy to American Liberty."

As was the case with Williamsburg merchant John Prentis, who had imprudently ordered the tea that got dumped into the river at Yorktown in November 1774, merchants such as John Hook were unusually well-known members of their communities, and suspicions directed at them were undoubtedly injurious to their businesses. Charges like those that Hook faced could sow seeds of distrust in a community and sometimes produced long-lasting animosities.

Hook evidently faced no further committee action against him in the spring and summer of 1775. He continued to operate his store for many years, even though he also continued to have reservations about the course of human events and did not always conceal his opinions. In October 1777, a mob forced him to sign an oath of allegiance to Virginia, which he had not voluntarily done. Still later, Hook was involved in a lawsuit that concerned, in part, payment that he claimed he was owed for two steers that the Continental Army had taken from him during the war.

Hook's court case apparently arose from some insufficiency in the documentation of his claim for reimbursement. The General Assembly authorized payment to men and women who had voluntarily furnished foodstuffs, horses, draft animals, cattle, wagons, or other needful supplies to the Continental Army; or, if the army requisitioned and took the supplies from people who did not remain loyal to the king, the law authorized compensation in much the same manner. The process required claimants to produce the receipts or other records that officers or commissaries gave them when they took supplies for the use of the army. The law required that county courts verify the claims and compile lists of all residents of the county who should be reimbursed and in what amounts. The county lists, called public service claims, served as the warrant for the state treasurer to authorize payment. For some reason, Hook believed that he was entitled to receive more than he did, or he had received nothing at all.

According to a local tradition, Patrick Henry, who was the opposing counsel at the trial, used knowledge of Hook's reluctant patriotism to good advantage. Henry contrasted Hook's behavior with that of the patriots at Valley Forge and elsewhere. His first biographer, William Wirt, recounted the story of Henry's argument in court: "He painted the distress of the American army, exposed almost naked to the rigour of a winter's sky, and marking the frozen ground over which they marched, with the blood of their unshod feet; where was the man, he said, who had an American heart in his bosom, who would not have thrown open his fields, his barns, his cellars, the doors of his house, the portals of his breast, to have received with open arms, the meanest"—least—"soldier in that little band of famished patriots?"

Wirt wrote that when Henry described to the court the surrender to George Washington's army at Yorktown, "the audience saw before their eyes the humiliation and dejection of the British, as they marched out of their trenches—they saw the triumph which lighted up every patriotic face, and heard the shouts of victory, and the cry of Washington and liberty, as it rung and echoed through the American ranks, and was reverberated from the hills and shores of the neighboring river." But "hark," Henry exclaimed, as Wirt reported the conclusion of the tale, "what notes of discord are these which disturb the general joy, and silence the acclamations of victory—they are the notes of *John Hook*, hoarsely bawling through the American camp, *beef! beef! beef!*"

Henry convulsed the courtroom with what was almost certainly a much-embellished story. The jury immediately returned with a verdict against Hook, who "began to hear around him a cry more terrible than that of *beef:* it was the cry of *tar and feathers:* from the application of which, it is said, that nothing saved him but a precipitate flight and the speed of his horse."

The politics of the American Revolution sowed seeds of community disruption throughout the country, and men such as Hook who expressed reservations sometimes suffered ostracism or even worse. Some of them, in fact, fled Virginia to England and in the process lost much or all of their American property. John Hook stayed, though, and ran his shop, which served the people of his community who continued to do business with him. He even later hired Patrick Henry to represent him in another lawsuit and told Henry at that time, "If you will only manage this case for me with the same energy and ability, as you did against me when you defeated the ends of Justice . . . we shall be sure to win."

Hook's experiences with the county committee and his neighbors teach us about the climate of public opinion far away from the towns and small cities of eastern Virginia about which we know more. His business records also teach us much about the operations of local economies in the Blue Ridge Mountains at the end of the eighteenth century and the beginning of the nineteenth, first in Bedford County and then to the south in Franklin County, where Hook later conducted his store. Historian Ann Smart Martin imaginatively used Hook's business records and others like them to illuminate that aspect of American commerce in her 2008 book, *Buying into the World of Goods: Early Consumers in Backcountry Virginia.*

6

Anthony Warwick, of Isle of Wight and Nansemond Counties

ANTHONY WARWICK AND MANY OTHER MEN had much more serious difficulties with county committees than did John Hook. Warwick was one of many British agents of tobacco trading firms and other mercantile houses who resided in Virginia and worked for, or managed the affairs of the employees of, the British firms. Warwick was well enough known in southeastern Virginia in 1774 and 1775 that his actions attracted attention beyond his neighborhood. He had been present in November 1774 when the colonial merchants association met with members of the House of Burgesses in Williamsburg and somebody put up a gallows and brought out a bucket of tar and some feathers. Warwick reportedly narrowly escaped violence then for his opposition to the politics of the colony's political leaders and his refusal to sign the Continental Association.

Warwick had also had a run-in with the Nansemond County Committee a few weeks later, when he took delivery of half a chest of East India Company tea from a ship that landed it in Norfolk. (The city of Suffolk absorbed Nansemond County in 1974.) He had hoped to sell the tea at a country store that he owned in North Carolina. When the committee confronted him with the charge that he had improperly and unpatriotically imported tea, Warwick and his local business partner reportedly signed the Continental Association "voluntarily" late in 1774.

That was just the beginning. "We hear from Isle of Wight," Williamsburg printer John Pinkney reported in his *Virginia Gazette* of August 24, 1775, "that a certain Anthony Warwick, being lately summoned to appear before the committee of Nansemond county, on a suspicion of having violated the association, in a letter addressed to that committee, declared he would not appear without a promise of protection from the people of Isle of Wight county, and in the said letter abused them in the most scurrilous manner; some worthy gentlemen of Nansemond immediately gave information thereof to the injured people. Upon which a number of respectable inhabitants of Isle of Wight assembled, and seized the said Anthony Warwick (he being in the neighbourhood) and conveyed him to Smithfield, where they detained him some time, in order that a committee might determine in what manner he ought to be dealt with; but a sufficient number of members not attending, and the said Warwick not giving any satisfactory reason for his illiberal abuse, the populace very deliberately led him to the stocks, and having prepared him for the purpose, gave him a fashionable suit of *tar and feathers,* being the most proper badge of distinction for men of his complexion. They then mounted him on a horse, and drove him out of town, through a shower of eggs, the smell of which, our correspondent informs us, seemed to have a material effect upon the delicate constitution of this *motleyed* gentleman. At parting, the gentlemen gave Mr. Warwick a friendly piece of advice, which it is hoped he will observe, if only for the sake of his own interest."

The newspaper report does not indicate why the Nansemond County Committee summoned Warwick to attend. The county was adjacent to Isle of Wight County, location of the town of Smithfield. It seems very likely that the committee had received word or had heard rumors that Warwick had purchased and shipped 600 barrels of pork to Boston for the British army there, although the date of the shipment is not reliably documented.

We know about the pork because Warwick mentioned it more than a decade later when he filed a claim with the American Loyalist Claims Commission for reimbursement of his American property that the governments of Virginia and North Carolina confiscated or sold at auction after he fled to the protection of the British army and navy. His claim, or memorial as it was called, is in Records of the American Loyalist Claims Commission, Audit Office, Series 12, volume 56, pages 227–28, Archives of the United Kingdom, formerly the Public Record Office (PRO).

In that claim, Warwick gave his own relation of the events in Nansemond and Isle of Wight Counties. He recalled, in the formal, third-person language of such claims, that he had joined the royal governor of Virginia, John Murray, fourth Earl of Dunmore, at the military encampment in or near Portsmouth in the summer of 1775, but went to Nansemond County to

"A New Method of MACARONY MAKING, as practised at BOSTON," ca. 1774. A coat of tar and feathers. In common English use then, the Italian word *macaroni* meant fancy, as in "stick a feather in your hat and call it macaroni." (Library of Congress, Prints & Photographs Division)

transact some business with a friend "concerning a very important affair." While there, "when he thought himself in perfect safety in the House of a Friend in whom he had full confdce. he found himself surrounded and surprised by a Multitude, who forcing open the House violently seized your Memst."—memorialist—"and regardless of his ill state of Health a merciless rabble dragged him, frequently by the Hair of his head the distance of ten Miles. Here after suffering tortures a Descriptn. of which would wound your Lordships feelings, Your Memst. was stript, even of his shirt tied to a public whipping post, and subjected to the shameful punishment of Tar and Feathers, in the presence of many hundred Spectators."

"Your Lordships Memst.," Warwick concluded, "having undergone this ignoms."—ignominious—"treatment, as the last blow of their insolence and malice was not allowed to clean himself or take any kind of Refreshment, but in the condition had his Cloaths put into, and was obliged to ride

15 Miles, the distance he was from Home. Your Memst. too in his Case had the farther Mortificatn. that his punishment was altogr. singular, he being the only instance of the sort in Virginia."

It was, indeed, a very painful thing to be smeared with hot, sticky tar and then to have feathers stuck to the tar, all of which was difficult to remove. The treatment that Warwick received was also humiliating. A few other recorded references to tarring and feathering in Virginia exist, but it is not clear whether the references are to actual events or to threats. It is possible that there were other instances.

Two letters that Anthony Warwick wrote while he was in Portsmouth or Norfolk in the autumn of 1775 were intercepted and handed to Virginia patriots, which implicated him even further as being fully in sympathy with other loyalists and even in assisting the king's forces. The letters are published on pages 235–36 and 368–71 in volume 4 of William J. Van Schreeven, Robert L. Scribner, and Brent Tarter, eds., *Revolutionary Virginia, The Road to Independence: A Documentary Record,* 7 vols. (Charlottesville, 1973–83). Sometime in 1776, Warwick was able to get aboard a ship and safely sail for England.

Some other loyalists had even greater difficulty than Warwick in leaving Virginia. John Agnew, who for about twenty-five years had been rector of a parish church in Nansemond County, was so outspoken in opposition to the local political leaders that in the spring of 1775 armed men blocked his access to the church and prohibited him from conducting services there. Agnew described what he called "the baneful Conseqcs. of Civil War" in the long memorial that he later submitted to the American Loyalist Claims Commission. He related that he had joined Lord Dunmore sometime in 1775, as Anthony Warwick had done. "About the 1st. of Feby. 1776," Agnew recalled, his wife "came privately into said Fleet with some provisions for her Husband and Son which were very scarce and your Memorialist having accompanied her a little way from the Shore was unfortunately seized by an Ambush and carried directly to prison."

Agnew testified that his captors "hurried him to a Guard House by a party of Soldiers where he was shut up three days in a small room with Sick and distempered Negroes and Sailors, without Bedding Fire or Wood." He slept there "in that severe Season with a Log of Wood for his pillow. Such cruel treatment being complained of by the Inhabitants he was at length removed to the County Jail Whilst imprisoned there the greatest part of his best Negroes were caught and with Slaves of other Loyalists forcibly sent off in Waggons of the Officers of the said Regiment with other plunder to their Settlements in the back County." Agnew spent about six months under arrest in the public jail in Williamsburg and along with his wife endured numerous hardships before they were finally able to flee Virginia.

7

College Camp

THE THIRD VIRGINIA CONVENTION, which met in July and August 1775, created a two-regiment army and appointed Patrick Henry commander in chief and colonel of the First Virginia Regiment. The first companies of soldiers, all volunteers, began to arrive in Williamsburg during the third week of September and set up camp near the College of William and Mary at what they called College Camp. On October 21, Colonel Henry assigned some of the companies to his First Virginia Regiment and the others to the Second Virginia Regiment, under the command of Colonel William Woodford.

The accounts of the organization and disciplining of the little army are preserved in one of the regimental orderly books, where daily orders for the Second Virginia Regiment were recorded. It later became the orderly book of the Eighth Virginia Regiment, which the Fourth Virginia Convention created in January 1776. The volume is in the Historical Society of Pennsylvania, and a microfilm copy is in the Library of Virginia. The orders for the Second Virginia Regiment were published serially as Brent Tarter, ed., "The Orderly Book of the Second Virginia Regiment, September 27, 1775–April, 1776," *Virginia Magazine of History and Biography* 85 (1977): 156–83, 302–36. The faulty spellings and punctuation in the orderly book entries are those of the orderly sergeants, who recorded the orders, not of the officers who issued them.

Creating an army out of almost nothing posed many challenges. Even though Colonel Henry and many of the officers had taken part in militia musters, none of them, with the exception of Colonel Woodford, were veterans of actual military service. They probably had not had much experience

Patrick Henry (1736–99), by George Bagby Matthews, ca. 1883, after Thomas Sully. (Virginia State Artwork Collection; Library of Virginia)

with the logistical and disciplinary problems that an army in the field faced; and the men under their command had no such experience at all.

On September 28, the orderly sergeant recorded in the orderly book some of the requirements that officers and men had to follow. "The Adjutant," he wrote, "is to Give the Captain or Commandant a form of Compys."—companies—"for making the Daily and General returns, & the Quartermasters Serjeants are to Give the forms of the Victualling Returns the Quartermasters Serjeant is also to Attend to having the Necessarys made." Victuals were articles of food; necessaries, or facilities for doing the necessities of nature, were latrines.

The orders for the day included instructions to keep the camp clean, "Also the kitchens for Cooking, and to Apply to Mister finnie"—Quartermaster William Finnie of Williamsburg—"for a Spade, Shovel & Ax, for Each Company as they Arrive in Town, also to Attend Mr. Finnie in Collecting the Necessary Camp Utensils for the Soldiers and Deliver them to the Captains." The orders directed the "men to be under arms Drelling and Training to the other Necessary Decipline from the hours of Ten O'Clock in the morning till half an Hour after twelve. Also after three for one Hour, or an Hour & a half, at which Times the long Rolls are to beat for Assembling the men."

The orders directed that the drummers and fifers teach the men the signals for maneuvers on a battlefield. Soldiers of the time depended on hearing rhythmic drum signals rather than voice commands in the noise of battle. Another order stated, "The Soldiers are not to Come into Town by any means without leave of the Commandant of their Companies and the Officers are not to allow above three or four to be Absent at one Time, & that not to be at the Time of any Duty."

On October 9, after the arrival of more companies, the orderly sergeant recorded more general directives. "The Victualling Returns to be made out by 2: OClock the Day before Drawing Provisions, to the Quartermaster, a Subaltern Officer of Each Company to be Attended by a man from Each Mess and they are to be at the Store House by sun rise in order to Draw provisions from the Commissary or his Agent who will be Ready to Issue them at that Time." And, "the Serjeants and Corporals not on Duty with their arms in proper Order are to Attend the Adjutant, Immediately after prayers, in order to be properly trained. The Quarter Guard to Mount Daily is to Consist of a Serjeant Corporal and 12 privates, and Order Serjeant with two Sentries, to Attend the Committee of Safety while Setting." The Committee of Safety was the committee that the Third Virginia Convention created to enforce the ordinances that it had passed and to serve as an executive body with command over the military. "It is particularly expected that Officers attend to the Arms of the Soldiers that they be Dried a[nd] Cleaned & have Good flints and kept in the Best order."

The orders for that day suggest that a certain amount of confusion or congestion, as might have been expected, attended the establishment and enlargement of College Camp because "The Health of the Soldiers Greatly Depends on the Cleanliness of the Camp, the Tents, Streets, and Entrenchments are to be Clean, the Necessary Houses to be Cleaned once in two Days, and the Camp Swept once every Day." Another order that day directed that "The Quarter Masters Sergeant and Camp Colourmen are to Collect all the Horns fit for Powder and Each Soldiers is to Mark his own Powderhorn, with all the Possible Expedition." And, "It is Expected that all Officers and Soldiers will preserve Decency and Good order in the Camp, and that Some irregularrity now practiced be Reformed with as much hast as young Recruits will admit of—"

On October 28, Colonel Woodford directed that the soldiers of the Second Virginia Regiment "are to attend the Camp Constantly & not Depart Without its Limits, Except with leave of a Commissioned Officer. Tis Observed with Concern that they Straggle into Town & are Disorderly there, this must not be Suffer'd"—permitted—"the masters of the College Complain of Depredations on their Guard Insolence & abuce of there Guardmen and that there Pasture, and an out house have been pulled Down by the soldiers, such Attention must be Given to prevent those Complaints in future, & the Soldiers warned at their perril to behave themselves in a Better manner for the future—"

The orders and regulations recorded in the orderly book of the Second Virginia Regiment resemble corresponding orders and regulations in other contemporary military records. They are a reminder that army life, as has frequently been described, consisted of hurrying up and then waiting, as well as long intervals of boredom interrupted by short bursts of terror. It was, and is, not glamorous heroics except for a few people for a few of those moments of terror during a battle.

The orderly book does not include information about the women who were almost always present with military units in those days. Women cooked, did laundry, mended uniforms, sometimes nursed ill or injured soldiers, and performed many necessary chores, often without any compensation other than the satisfaction that they gained from serving their country. Some of those women were undoubtedly wives of soldiers, but probably not wives of officers. Women who followed army encampments from place to place during wartime and did that necessary work were called camp followers, a term that in many people's minds later came to signify prostitutes, or sex workers. Some of them undoubtedly performed in that role, or in addition to their other traditional roles. Camp followers were not all prostitutes or merely prostitutes; they were valuable adjuncts to the fighting men.

One thing that we can glimpse from the orderly book is that large concentrations of soldiers placed burdens on civilian populations near an encampment or the scene of a battle. The army needed meat, grain, and vegetables and fruits in season; cloth and leather to make or repair uniforms and other equipment; draft animals and wagons for hauling supplies; and horses for infantry officers and cavalry units. Properly supplying the armies of the United States during the War for Independence posed constant challenges, and men like Quartermaster William Finnie were among the most important people who worked to keep the army fed, clothed, and equipped.

Camp life could be boring and difficult. When the Second Virginia Regiment was stationed at the Great Bridge, just south of Norfolk, close to the naval and military forces of the royal governor and his loyalist supporters,

Colonel Woodford acknowledged the difficulties in the orders of the day for December 6, 1775. "The Commanding Officer is very sensible of the great Fatigues and hardships that the Troops Necessarily suffer in Winter Campaigns in this Disagreeable Country & the Delays that Attend our Opperations in the present situation of our Innemies he does therefore Humbly Recommend it to all Officers & Soldiers to bear them with patients as it is hoped that they will not continue long."

Woodford also reminded the men under his command that "we are the Body of men our Country at present Depends upon for protection against our Unnatril Ennamies," unnatural in that two armed bodies of subjects of the same king were facing each other under conditions that could lead to a battle. "If any soldier thinks himself agreaved in any Respect Upon Applycation to the Commanding Officer it shall be redres'd if in his power, and ever thing made as Comfortable as our present Situation admits of, the men of Duty to strick their Tents, dry their Ground, Clean their streats and about their Camp and pitch them again before sunset—"

One order of the day for December 7, 1775, concerned a court martial that met to hear and decide charges against some of the soldiers. The very brief record of the court martial in the regimental orderly book lists the names of the officers of the court. One of them was a young lieutenant in the Culpeper Minutemen, a company of volunteers who had enlisted with the understanding that they could be called into the field anywhere at a moment's notice. The name of the lieutenant was John Marshall, who that day took part in a judicial proceeding for the very first time. He later served for thirty-four years as chief justice of the United States.

On December 8, the day before a surprise attack from the governor's forces, the orderly book recorded, "The Quartermaster has had necessary Houses made in the rear Sufficient for all the men where they are expresly ordered for the future to ease themselves and not to Do it about the Camp all Sentinals are To take notice of this order and as they see any man Disobeying it they are to take him prisoner and send him to the guard—When ever the weather clears up the whole Tents in the Camp to be struck and every man off Duty to be Imployed in Cleaning up all the filth in and about their Camp and Houses to this it is hoped the Officers as well as the Serjt. will attend as the present nastiness will be a short Time"—in a short time—"Bread some Infectious Disorders amounghts us."

Nothing comparable to a modern weather bureau existed in the eighteenth century, and no newspapers published regular reports of weather conditions, so it is only rarely that references such as this to when the weather "clears up" allow us to know when and where soldiers lived and worked in cold or wet and muddy circumstances, in unpleasant conditions described as the "present nastiness." The colder and wetter the conditions, the more the men needed firewood to keep warm and to cook their rations. Soldiers who foraged for wood as well as for foodstuffs disrupted all neighborhoods in which armies marched or were stationed and placed unanticipated heavy burdens on civilian residents. Foraging parties could also contribute unintentionally to civilian resentment or even disaffection from the cause for which the soldiers enlisted. Enterprising men and women sometimes acquired supplies and sold them to the army, which made the civilians some money and also enabled them to contribute to the cause.

8

The Battle of Great Bridge

THE FIRST MAJOR MILITARY ENGAGEMENT of the War for Independence in Virginia occurred on December 9, 1775, at a river crossing known as the Great Bridge, south of the port city of Norfolk. Governor John Murray, fourth Earl of Dunmore, had his military headquarters near Norfolk, and the Second Virginia Regiment was stationed at the Great Bridge to prevent his army from maneuvering freely in the southeastern corner of Virginia. Several companies of minutemen, so-called because they had volunteered to be ready to march at a moment's notice, reinforced the Second Virginia Regiment, and a small number of North Carolina volunteers had recently joined the Virginians. An additional volunteer reinforcement from North Carolina was then on the way to the Great Bridge. The total number of armed American men at the Great Bridge camp that day was almost 900.

The governor's forces, under command of Captain Charles Fordyce, included an estimated 200 regular army soldiers, loyalist volunteers whom the governor designated the Queen's Own Loyal Virginia Regiment, and Black men, whom the governor designated as Lord Dunmore's Ethiopian Regiment, who volunteered to fight for the king and against white Virginians after Dunmore in November had promised them their freedom if they did. Colonel William Woodford, in command of the Virginia forces, estimated that Fordyce had about 500 men altogether. Few or none of them, with the possible exception of some of Fordyce's British soldiers, had ever been in a battle.

Woodford reported on the battle in a letter to the president of the Fourth Virginia Convention, which was then meeting in Williamsburg, but the best description of the actual fighting is in a letter that one of the officers,

Richard Kidder Meade, wrote on December 18. It was published in Charles Campbell, ed., *The Bland Papers: Being a Selection from the Manuscripts of Colonel Theodorick Bland, Jr., of Prince George County, Virginia, to Which are Prefixed an Introduction, and a Memoir of Colonel Bland,* 2 vols. (Petersburg, 1840–43), 1:38–39.

"I will give you the circumstances of the battle," Meade wrote to a friend. "A servant lad, without cause, deserted from our minute officers, and fell in with the enemy, who questioned him as to our numbers, &c.; he said, not exceeding 30. The governor, pleas'd with this account, and sure of success, muster'd his whole force, which march'd in the night to the fort, with orders to force our breastworks early next morning, or die in the attempt."

The governor did not accompany the men, and it may very well be doubted that Meade understood correctly that the servant had estimated the size of the combined Virginia–North Carolina force at a mere 30. Dunmore, Meade believed, ignorant of how many Virginia and North Carolina volunteers he faced and believing that they were ill-prepared for fighting, had "taught his troops to believe that we shou'd not stand more than one fire, and from report, that shou'd we conquer, no quarter wou'd be given." By that, he meant that Dunmore anticipated that the Virginians would probably give up after "one fire," but that if they somehow prevailed, they would treat the British harshly and without mercy, or "quarter."

Early in the morning of December 9, Meade continued his description, before "the men were out of our tents, the firing began; at first it pass'd as our usual sport—an exchange of a few morning guns; but the alarm soon took, and as they advanc'd the bullets whistled on every side; it is impossible by letter to give you a full description; but their advance was along a causeway six abreast; a small guard com[manded]"—the square brackets and the letters they enclose are in the printed text, either to expand an abbreviation or to replace torn letters—"at our breastwork began the fire, who were soon reinforc'd, tho' then inferior in numbers; at this time, (tho' for the smoak I did not see it,) the enemy fell back a little, but soon rally'd, by the vast bravery of Capt. Forydce, who march'd with many bullets through him, within twenty yards of the breast-work, before he fell, when the few remains of his noble followers retreated, falling as they went, by the management of Colonel Stevens"—Lieutenant Colonel Edward Stevens, of the Culpeper Minutemen—"who flank'd them with a hand-full of riflemen; in short, the like is not to be equall'd in history; they fought, bled, and died, like Englishmen, and, I have the pleasure to say, were treated as such." Meade concluded his account of the battle: "The scene, when the dead and wounded were bro't off, was too much; I then saw the horrors of war in perfection, worse than can be imagin'd; 10 and 12 bullets thro' many; limbs broke in 2 or 3 places; brains turning out. Good God, what a sight!"

With "they fought, bled, and died, like Englishmen," Meade not only praised the bravery of Captain Fordyce and the men who fought under his command but exhibited his own pride in their shared heritage. Colonel Woodford wrote about the English attackers in almost the same words. The Americans honored the gallantry of their adversaries. They did not yet regard themselves as enemies of the English, merely as defenders of their own English rights and liberties in America.

Woodford counted twelve soldiers who perished with Fordyce and reported to the convention that he had taken seventeen prisoners. He believed that the British probably suffered about fifty casualties, including dead, wounded, and captured. Of Woodford's command, only "one Man of ours Wounded in the Hand."

A few days after the battle, Dunmore withdrew his military force from Norfolk. As additional North Carolina companies arrived soon thereafter to reinforce Woodford, a considerable party of loyalists took refuge aboard royal warships in the Elizabeth River or in the nearby town of Portsmouth. Woodford's combined Virginia and North Carolina army then occupied Norfolk.

9

The Great Distress of Peter Anderson and Shadrack Furman

PETER ANDERSON FOUGHT AT the Great Bridge, too, but on the other side from Richard Kidder Meade. We know this because sometime about 1783, Anderson submitted a memorial to the British government. It is preserved on page 13, Series 1, volume 1018, of the records of the War Office in the Archives of the United Kingdom, formerly the Public Record Office (PRO).

Anderson related in his claim for reimbursement of lost property that he was one of several free Black residents of Norfolk in 1775 and that he enlisted in the Black regiment that Governor John Murray, fourth Earl of Dunmore, recruited after he issued a proclamation of martial law in November 1775 and promised freedom to enslaved Virginians who fought for the king and against their masters. At the time that Anderson submitted his memorial, he described himself as "being in great Distress."

Anderson testified that he had willingly enlisted "under Lord Dunmore & was Always ready & willing when call'd for & was at the Battle at the great Bridge in Virginea when 350 Grenideers & 100 Blacks fought 1600 Americans." He related that he was captured "& in great Danger of His Life when he got out of the Garrett Window" and escaped. As a result of Anderson's having loyally fought against the Virginians, he "Lost his all," including "4 Beds & Furniture 20 Head of Hogs 4 Chests of Cloath."

The petition is confusing as to the sequence of some of the events because the sentences alternately but briefly relate his experiences and itemize some of his losses as a consequence. Anderson continued that "he was six Months in Prison & six Months in the Woods & then Enter'd into His Britinack Majesty's service again." Anderson concluded, "I am A free Man

& willing to serve His Majesty again But having Nothing to Subsist on he hopes your Honor's will allow Him some Support His Age is 38 Years."

It is unclear what compensation or reward Anderson received as a result of his loyalty to the king and his service and losses. Nor is it clear what relief, if any, Shadrack Furman received for his even greater sacrifices after he dictated and made his mark on a petition in the autumn of 1787. He asked that it be addressed to no less a personage than William Pitt, who is often called William Pitt the Younger because he was the son of William Pitt, also called the Great Commoner, who served as first minister during the war with France in the 1760s. William Pitt the Younger was then the chancellor of the exchequer and the king's first minister. Furman's petition is in the records of the Audit Office, Series 13, volume 29, folder D, the Archives of the United Kingdom.

"The humble petition of Shadrack Furman Sheweth, That your petitioner was a free black man and lived in Acamack County in America"—Accomack County, Virginia, the northern of the two counties on the Eastern Shore, the peninsula between Chesapeake Bay and the Atlantic Ocean—"at the Commencement of the late Troubles in very good Circumstances and on Account of his Attachment to the British Government rendered himself inimical to the rebels." He apparently lived there until after the British invasion of 1780. "That the rebels getting Information of his entertaining some of the British Troops in his House and otherwise supplying them with provisions when they first came into Virginia, they on the first of January 1781 burnt destroyed or carried away the property of many Loyalists and the whole" of his "Effects." Furman attached an inventory that itemized property worth £146 19s 9d "and upwards." The itemized property list is no longer with the petition.

Furman recalled that "Shortly afterwards in order to extort Intelligence from petitioner respecting the British Troops he was Seized by the rebels and after dangerously wounding him in divers parts, the Marks of which petr. can still shew, they stripped tied up and gave him 500 Lashes and then left him almost dead in the Field by reason of which your Honors petitioner lost his Eye Sight, and the use of one of his Legs by a stroke of an Axe they gave him, and his Health is otherwise so much impaired from the wounds in his Head received from them, that he is sometimes bereft of reason."

That was only the beginning. "That soon after the aforesaid ill Treatment," Furman continued, "& as soon as your petr. got a little strength and dreading further ill usage from the Rebels petr. went on Board of a privateer"—a private ship armed and operated as a warship under authority of the British Navy—"where he Joined the British army and . . . rendered himself as useful as possible until his Situation from the aforesaid ill Treatment rendered it necessary to send him to Head Quarters under the Care of the General Doctors." He was eventually discharged as unfit for duty. Furman and his wife somehow managed to reach London in the spring of 1787, and he dictated his petition that autumn.

"May it please your Honor," Furman concluded, "to take your petitioners case into Consideration and as your Petitioner and wife are from a comfortable Situation in Life reduced to the lower Ebb of poverty and Distress on account of his Loyalty and Attachmt. to His majesty be pleased to order that some provision or support may be Granted to your petr. and wife who are now entirely depending on the Charity of the public having neither Friends Credit or Money—"

Anderson and Furman had been free men, but most Black Virginians were enslaved when the War for Independence began. A great many enslaved Virginians fled their places of residence and attempted to join the British during the war. The exact number is not known and is, in fact, the subject of some scholarly debate, rooted in part on an unsubstantiated estimate that Thomas Jefferson later made that he may have extrapolated from the proportion of his own enslaved people who disappeared from his plantations during the war. The number was definitely large, though. It is likely that more Black Virginians died fighting for the king during the war than died fighting for the liberty of other, mostly white, Americans; and it is possible that more died attempting to join the British than succeeded. Some men, women, and their children made it to Nova Scotia and settled on the coast of that British colony, and others eventually settled in Africa, but a very large number of people who sought to join the British did not make it out of Virginia.

British warships in the Elizabeth River in 1776 and later at anchor in various places in Chesapeake Bay took on board as many refugees as they could, but many of the refugees apparently died violently as they tried to join the British or of disease on the ships. Naval officers tossed dead bodies into the bay at night, not unlike how captains of slave-trading ships had tossed overboard the bodies of men, women, and children who died at sea en route from Africa to lifetime slavery in the Americas. Most of the people who attempted to escape from slavery in Virginia apparently failed.

In 1796, a visitor to Norfolk saw that "Many Waggon loads of the bones of Men women and Children, stripped of the flesh by Vultures and Hawks which abound here, covered the sand for a most considerable length. . . . The hopes of getting on board the English fleet collected them at the mouth of the Chesapeak bay, they were left behind in thousands and perished. Children died sucking the breasts of their dead mothers, and Women feeding upon the corpses of their starved children. The remnants of decaying rags still point to the skeletons of many of these miserable victims."

10

Mary Webley and Her Miserable Little Children

IN OCTOBER 1776, MARY WEBLEY submitted a petition to the House of Delegates, as the lower House of the General Assembly of the independent Commonwealth of Virginia was called, because of what had happened to her and her family on the first day of January 1776.

During the colonial period and until long after the American Civil War, the government of Virginia had no general laws and no established bureaucracy by which people could obtain relief of the sort that Webley and her family desperately needed. People therefore petitioned the General Assembly for aid. Petitioning was an ancient right that English kings had long recognized and that was common in the colonies. The process as it existed in Virginia required that on a court day, when the county court met and a large number of people would be present, the petitioner post a notice at the courthouse of an intent to petition and stating the purpose of the petition. That allowed anybody who wished to support or oppose the petition to take action, such as present a counterpetition.

The forms of petitions were standardized. From the earliest times when people submitted petitions to the king, they were always in the third person and opened with a statement of the humble status of the petitioner and closed with a prayer that the request of the petitioner be granted. (Memorials for relief that Anthony Warwick, John Agnew, Peter Anderson, Shadrack Furman, and the other loyalists submitted to the British government were very similar in format.) Because the House of Delegates, which received petitions to the General Assembly, probably would not have accepted one that was not in proper form, most people needed the assistance of an experienced legislator, a lawyer, or a county clerk to follow the customary and legal forms for presenting petitions. Nearly all of the petitions submitted before the 1770s were lost when most of the legislative archive was destroyed during one of the British raids into Virginia late in the War for Independence.

The House of Delegates received the petition of Mary Webley on October 11, 1776. One of the delegates from the city of Norfolk or from Norfolk County probably presented it. Legally, Norfolk was then a borough, not a city, a distinction of nomenclature without any practical difference. The petition is preserved in the Records of the General Assembly, Legislative Petitions, Norfolk Borough, Record Group 78, Library of Virginia. The Speaker of the House of Delegates referred it to the proper committee for consideration. The many thousands of petitions in the state archives can be viewed online by clicking on Legislative Petitions in the site index to the library's website at lva.virginia.gov.

The petition begins, "To the Honourable the Speaker and Gentlemen of the House of Delegates The Petition of the unfortunate Mary Webley late a Resident of the Borough of Norfolk humbly sheweth,

"That your Petitioner on new Years Day last, while suckling her Child the youngest of three now dependent on her, had her Leg broken by a Cannon Ball from the Liverpool Man of War." HMS *Liverpool* was one of several warships that the British had sent to Virginia to assist Governor Dunmore to put down the opposition of the colonists. The governor may have then been living on one of the ships, perhaps aboard the largest, HMS *William,* after he and his forces abandoned Norfolk following the defeat of the British attack that he ordered on the American emplacement at the Great Bridge, south of Norfolk.

Early in the morning of January 1, 1776, the warships fired some cannonballs into the city and started several fires. Virginia and North Carolina soldiers, still drunk from the night before or already drunk celebrating the new year, then set fire to the residences and places of business of local loyalists. (The officers may have even encouraged them.) They broke open casks of alcohol and drank it. They were completely out of control, with the result that almost the entire city burned, including the home of Mary Webley and her family.

She continued her narration of their sufferings: "That her Husband from the Loss of his right arm upwards of twenty Years since is scarcely able to maintain himself.

"That She hath at present no Ways or Means to procure Shelter or acquire Subsistence for herself and miserable little Children, her Husband and Self having had all their Effects totally destroyed in the Flames of Norfolk from whence they have been drove in most distresful Circumstances."

She "Therefore prays this honourable House will on Consideration of the Premises grant unto her such Aid and Relief as in their justice and mercy shall seem right." The General Assembly awarded Webley £10, not enough to support her, her disabled husband, and their miserable little children for an extended period, but enough, perhaps, to allow them to begin their lives again somewhere else or to rent or buy a residence in Norfolk when the city should be rebuilt. Later, the General Assembly provided additional relief for patriotic residents of the city whose property burned in the fire.

The soldiers and army officers knew who was responsible for the fire of January 1, 1776, as did the members of the Fourth Virginia Convention, who were then meeting in Williamsburg, but they concealed that information until the autumn of the year and let Americans elsewhere believe, falsely, that the British had destroyed the largest city in Virginia. Norfolk had about 6,000 residents on the day of the fire and was the eighth largest city in the English colonies of North America. That false belief was one of many factors during the first months of 1776 that caused a large proportion of colonists to decide that in such a war with the forces of their own king, they should declare independence.

Mary Webley was not the only resident of Norfolk who petitioned for relief, nor was she the only Virginia woman who petitioned on behalf of her family. In November 1777, Martha Hodges, of York County, submitted a petition that recited that her husband "John Hodges entered into the Minute service where he caught a cold that brought on a disorder which occasiond his death, leaving a Waggon & Team which is the principle support of your Petitioner & her children. That some time in the Month of September last Colo. Joseph Cabell impressed your Petitioners said Waggon Team & driver to remove the Baggage of his Militia to Wms:burg & after keeping the said Waggon & Team eight days & doing great damage to the Team he paid your Petitioner £4 only, being half the price per day your Petitioner was at that time offerd for the said Waggon & Team."

But that was not all. "That some short time afterwards your Petitioners said Waggon & Team were again impressed" by a militia officer "to remove

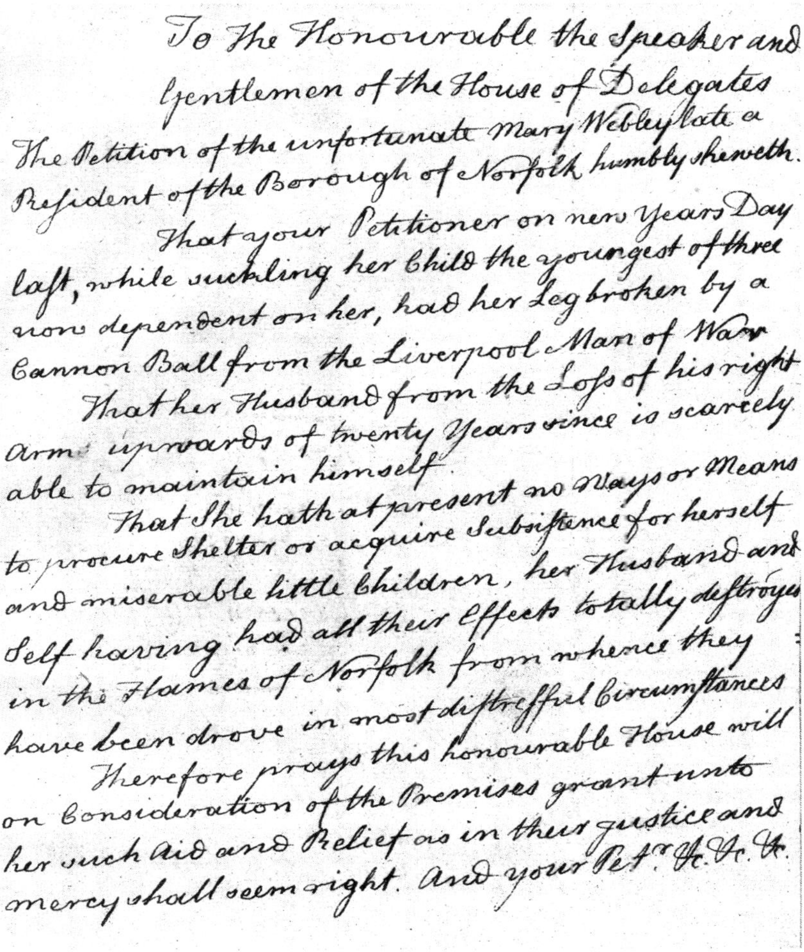
To The Honourable the Speaker and
Gentlemen of the House of Delegates
The Petition of the unfortunate Mary Webley late a
Resident of the Borough of Norfolk humbly sheweth.
That your Petitioner on new Years Day
last, while suckling her Child the youngest of three
now dependent on her, had her Leg broken by a
Cannon Ball from the Liverpool Man of War
That her Husband from the Loss of his right
arm upwards of twenty Years since is scarcely
able to maintain himself.
That She hath at present no Ways or Means
to procure Shelter or acquire Subsistence for herself
and miserable little Children, her Husband and
Self having had all their Effects totally destroyed
in the Flames of Norfolk from whence they
have been drove in most distressful Circumstances
Therefore prays this honourable House will
on Consideration of the Premises grant unto
her such Aid and Relief as in their justice and
mercy shall seem right. And your Petr. &c. &c. &c.

Petition of Mary Webley to the General Assembly, October 1776. (Library of Virginia)

the Baggage" of the militia of Fluvanna County "& detaind them 19 days." The officer paid Hodges 18 shillings, 2 shillings less than a pound. Hodges concluded "That your Petitioner Humbly concieves her Country to be justly indebted to her the Balance of £13.10.4"—13 pounds, 10 shillings, 4 pence—"as your Petitioner could at those Time & have since actually hired her said Waggon & Team" for 20 shillings, or 1 pound, a day.

Families as well as soldiers were casualties or victims of war. Fewer women and children than men died as a direct result of fighting on battlefields, but every man killed, disabled, or weakened by illness caught in the service had dependent family members who, like Martha Hodges's family, lost their principal means of support. The surviving files of petitions to the Virginia General Assembly contain many more accounts of civilian hardship that the War for Independence created, not to mention petitions from veterans who also needed financial assistance from the public they had served.

Shortly after Martha Hodges presented her petition in November 1777, three women from another county submitted petitions that are all in the same handwriting of their male amanuensis. Some of the language is very similar, too. Anne Matthews, widow of Owen Matthews, recited that he had joined the army and marched to "New York & there died in the Month of March last, leaving your poor Petitioner with four small Children destitute of every necessary of Life."

The assembly received the other two petitions on a day in December. "The Petition of Hannah Moody Widow of Samuel Moody humbly sheweth that her Husband having inlisted as a Soldier" had also marched to the north and died there, "leaving your poor Petitioner with three small Children in very deploreable circumstances."

Also, "The Petition of Mourning Savidge Widow of Philip Savidge humbly sheweth that her Husband" also enlisted and "marched to the Northward & there died, leaving your poor Petitioner with two small Children destitute of every necessary of Life."

And on, and on, and on for years. Such is the result of war in all times and in all places. The General Assembly sometimes granted temporary relief for individual widows and orphans of soldiers or seamen who died or were permanently disabled during the war, but the state government created no permanent organization to aid the suffering veterans and their families.

11

No Inducement for a Poor Man to Fight

On February 29, 1776, Lund Washington wrote a long letter on several subjects to his cousin, General George Washington. The letter is in the George Washington Papers, Library of Congress, and has been published in Philander D. Chase et al., eds., *The Papers of George Washington, Revolutionary Series* (Charlottesville, 1985–), 3:393–98. A small part of the letter is an angry complaint about James Cleveland, of Loudoun County, on the Potomac River northwest of Mount Vernon. Both Washingtons knew Cleveland. In the letter, Lund Washington had some very harsh things to say about Cleveland.

Lund Washington informed his cousin: "Cleveland I am told has turn'd Polititian and is setg all Loudon together by the Ears, the Consequence of which will be I hope the loss of his life for I woud wish every Damn'd Vilian who meddles in matters he knows nothing off, may get Hang'd.—He says the Tennants shoud not pay Rents—the pay of officers and Soldiers shoud be the same, or what woud be still better they shoud not be paid at all, there is no inducement for a poor Man to Fight, for he has nothing to defend, let us go and Fight the Battle at once, and not be Shilly Shally, in this way, until all the Poor people are ruined—and such like Stuff that vexes me even to relate—I suppose the first Battle we have in this part of the Country will be in Loudon against General Cleveland for he has the Honour of being at the head of the Party."

The first recruitment acts and ordinances that the Third Virginia Convention adopted in August 1775 when it created the two-regiment army included a schedule for payment of officers and soldiers. It resembled laws that the General Assembly had passed during earlier wars and also earlier pay schedules for the British army. High-ranking officers, who were likely to be from families that were more prominent and prosperous than average, received much more than enlisted soldiers. Colonels received 25 shillings (£1 5s) a day and lieutenant colonels half that; majors received 10 shillings, captains 6, and lieutenants 4; but private soldiers received a mere 1 shilling and 4 pence, or a little more than 5 percent of what a colonel received and 22 percent of what a lieutenant received.

The inequality should not be surprising in a hierarchical society and in an even more hierarchical military. Some men like "General Cleveland" strenuously objected, and Cleveland more so than most. That some men complained about the differences between the pay of the various grades of officers and enlisted men should perhaps not be surprising, but Cleveland went much further to insist that all men receive the same pay, which was probably unique in Virginia. Nobody of note in Virginia then was ready for that kind of social democracy or equality, even if it were limited to white men, alone.

Complaints about the recruitment acts and terms of service cropped up regularly in Virginia throughout the War for Independence and from nearly every part of the state. Not long after Lund Washington reported on James Cleveland's incendiary actions in Loudoun County, 224 men in Lunenburg County, more than 150 miles to the south, signed a petition that the Fifth Virginia Convention received early in May 1776. It is preserved in the Papers of the Fifth Virginia Convention, Record Group 2, Library of Virginia, and has been published in William J. Van Schreeven, Robert L. Scribner, and Brent Tarter, eds., *Revolutionary Virginia, The Road to Independence: A Documentary Record,* 7 vols. (Charlottesville, 1973–83), 6:474–77.

The handwriting, spelling, and syntax in the torn and frayed document are not those of an educated man, and the words should perhaps be read aloud to bring out the sense and smooth over the rough edges. The complaint in the petition is in some respects more broadly egalitarian even than James Cleveland's demand that all men in the army be paid the same amount. It begins, "The Petition of the freeholders & Sundry of the Inhabitants of the County of Lunenburg." That informed members of the convention that some of the petitioners were landowners—"freeholders"—and that others of them were lesser "inhabitants" who probably worked as paid agricultural laborers or perhaps were artisans such as blacksmiths, coopers, or carpenters. It is clear from the body of the petition that not one of them was a large-scale planter or owner of a large number of enslaved laborers.

The 224 petitioners, "being deeply Empress'd with a tender Sense & feeling for the distresses of his Majesty's good Subjects in this & the rest of the Colonies & Provinces on the Continent hath hitherto Shown a readiness & Steadiness in Complying with the several resolves & Ordinances of your hon[ourable] Body, yet Mr. President our Circumstances & Situation at present is Such, that we must Observe (tho' its with Sorrow & reluctance) that by an Ordinance of Convention made in December last" for enlarging the Virginia army from two regiments to nine, "by which the Several Overseers are Exempted from bearing Arms in the Militia, & also Excus'd from being Drafted, as Soldiers, From this Indulgence many persons are become Overseers that Otherways wou'd not, on purpose to Secure themselves from Fighting in defence of their Country as well as their own property."

The Lunenburg County petitioners believed that the exemption was unjustified and would produce unjust consequences. "Many of your Petitioners are poor men with Families that are Incapable of Supporti[ng th]emsleves without Our labour & Assistance," they explained, "and we look up[on] it to be extremly hard & no ways [*one or two words torn*] that we Should be Obliged to leave our Farms [*one or two words torn*] him that if ever we Shou'd return again Wou'd find our Wives & Children dispers'd up & down the Country abeging, or at home aSlaving, and at the same time quite unable to help them to the Necessaries of life while the Overseers are aliving in ease & Affluence at the Expence of their Employers. For these, and many Other reasons that may be Assigned," the petitioners asked that the provision in the ordinance that exempted overseers from military service "may be repealed, or so amended, that they may be Obliged to bear Arms, and no ways Secur'd from being drafted as Soldiers."

The fifth and last of the Revolutionary Conventions that guided the process of converting the royal colony of Virginia into an independent American state did not grant the plea of the Lunenburg County men, nor did it heed (or even officially learn about) what James Cleveland had said. Instead, the government of the state and the Continental Congress both strove to stimulate enlistment by offering bonuses, called bounties, and eventually warrants that entitled soldiers to claim grants of western land that they could sell or where they could resettle after their terms of service concluded.

Nevertheless, throughout the war, the government of Virginia encountered difficulties in filling the requisitions of Congress for more soldiers for longer terms of service. Late in 1780, the House of Delegates went so far as to give preliminary approval to a draft bill that would have taken one in every twenty enslaved people from the holdings of wealthy planters for distribution to men who enlisted in the army for the duration of the war. On second or third thought, the delegates reversed themselves and did no such thing. But that they even considered it seriously is an indication of how difficult recruitment had become, how desperate some legislators may have been, and how disruptive or even revolutionary some proposals were.

James Cleveland was just the first, so far as we know. His assertion that "there is no inducement for a poor Man to Fight, for he has nothing to defend" appeared dangerous to Lund Washington as well as to his cousin, the general, and to many other Virginians. Land ownership was the basis of economic security for families and a prerequisite for men to be able to vote. Without owning land, as Cleveland indicated, men did not have much or anything else of value, in their society as it existed at the time, that was worth risking their lives except their own personal liberty. Ownership of land and also ownership of enslaved men, women, and children gave some men advantages over other men, which the petitioners from Lunenburg County pointed out. Together, these two documents disclose that as was almost always the case, people could perceive a rich man's war and a poor man's fight.

From the number of times that Virginia men complained about terms of enlistment, pay rates, and conditions of service, we have to conclude that however eager many Virginians may have appeared to be to take part at the beginning of the war, as it grew longer and longer they became more and more reluctant to take the dangerous step of going into the army without better inducements.

12

The Revolutionary Language of Liberty

When George Mason sat down in Williamsburg in May 1776 to compose the first draft for the Virginia Declaration of Rights, and when Thomas Jefferson sat down in Philadelphia in June 1776 to compose the first draft for the Declaration of Independence, they could have begun with some truly memorable words. Both of them could have written, "Four score and seven years ago"; they did not, but they could have. Four score and seven years later, when Abraham Lincoln wrote the first sentence of his Gettysburg Address, he used those words to remind Americans of all that they knew and all that they needed to know about the American Revolution and the representative democracy that it brought into being.

Mason and Jefferson could have used the same words for the same purpose, to remind Americans of all that they knew and all that they needed to know about the liberties of Englishmen as established at the time of the Glorious Revolution of 1689, when England adopted its Bill of Rights. It was to protect those rights and liberties that American men reluctantly chose to become independent in 1776 and to fight against their king.

The Declaration of Rights and the Declaration of Independence are two of the most important state papers of the memorable year 1776, two of the most influential documents in all of American history. Almost from the very beginning, Virginians and other Americans have regarded those documents as fundamental texts of American liberty, as if they endowed people with rights and protected people in the exercise of their liberties. In fact, however, the Virginia Declaration of Rights did not get incorporated into the state constitution until 1864, and the Declaration of Independence has never been part of the Constitution of the United States.

George Mason (1725–1792). (Library of Virginia)

Thomas Jefferson (1743–1826). (Library of Virginia)

People, however, generally considered both declarations as if they always were of constitutional status. Indeed, the word *constitution* as it was used at the time of the American Revolution encompassed all of the governmental institutions, practices, and beliefs under which the country functioned, not just one document that described governmental institutions, which is the modern meaning of the word. In the Gettysburg Address, Abraham Lincoln elevated the Declaration of Independence into iconic status as defining the essential meanings of the nation and of the national constitution that was ratified in 1788, a nation dedicated to the proposition that all men were created equal, that they were entitled to life, liberty, and the pursuit of happiness, and that they lived under a government of the people, by the people, and for the people.

We treat those documents, together with the Bill of Rights, which Americans added to their national constitution in 1791, as our sacred texts of liberty. We refer to the rights and liberties they enumerated as our individual and collective birthrights. George Mason and Thomas Jefferson, though, almost certainly did not intend for the Virginia Declaration of Rights and the Declaration of Independence to serve that broad a purpose in 1776. The documents were in part political propaganda designed to persuade members of the political nation—adult white men who owned real estate—to join together in an act of mass treason against their king.

The documents provide an excellent example of the workings of the law of unintended consequences. Almost everybody will recognize the most famous part of the Declaration of Independence: "that all men are created equal, that they are endowed by their Creator with certain unalienable Rights, that among these are Life, Liberty, and the pursuit of Happiness." Fewer people know the even more expansive corresponding words from the Declaration of Rights: "THAT all men are by nature equally free and independent, and have certain inherent rights, of which, when they enter into a state of society, they cannot, by any compact, deprive or divest their posterity; namely, the enjoyment of life and liberty, with the means of acquiring and possessing property, and pursuing and obtaining happiness and safety." Virginians have a constitutionally protected right to obtain happiness and safety, not merely to pursue happiness alone.

The Virginia Convention of May–July 1776, which instructed Virginia's delegates in Congress to introduce a resolution of independence and adopted the Declaration of Rights, amended the first article of the draft declaration to protect white Virginians' right to hold Black Virginians in slavery. Mason's draft began: "THAT all men are born equally free and independent, and have certain inherent natural rights, of which they cannot, by any compact, deprive or divest their posterity. . . ." The amended provision reads: "THAT all men are by nature equally free and independent, and have certain inherent rights, of which, when they enter into a state of society, they cannot, by any compact, deprive or divest their posterity; namely, the enjoyment of life and liberty, with the means of acquiring and possessing property, and pursuing and obtaining happiness and safety."

As members of the convention understood the amended language that they adopted, according to convention delegate Edmund Randolph, who was also the first attorney general of the state, "slaves, not being constituent members of our society, could never pretend to any benefit from such a maxim" that they had been born equally free and independent as white Virginians and entitled to liberty.

The convention also amended the final article in Mason's draft declaration. The original had contained a general statement of religious toleration, but delegate James Madison, then serving in his first elective office, drafted an amendment to change the section to make it state that "all men are equally entitled to the full and free exercise of it"—religion—"accord[g] to the dictates of Conscience; and therefore that no man or class of men ought on account of religion to be invested with peculiar emoluments or privileges; nor subjected to any penalties or disabilities."

Madison's proposed amendment provoked a debate because some convention delegates feared that it would weaken the official status of the Church of England as a part of the government. Madison then proposed a revision, which the delegates adopted. As amended the final article of the Virginia Declaration of Rights stated boldly, and without threatening the status and role of the Church of England in Virginia, "That religion, or the duty which we owe to our CREATOR, and the manner of discharging it, can be directed only by reason and conviction, not by force or violence, and therefore all men are equally entitled to the free exercise of religion, according to the dictates of conscience; and that it is the mutual duty of all to practice Christian forbearance, love, and charity towards each other."

That provision in the Virginia Declaration of Rights was the first of its kind in North America or almost anywhere. It was the direct precursor of the first portion of the First Amendment of the United States Bill of Rights that has been interpreted as granting all people full liberty to believe, or not believe, and to worship, or not worship, as they pleased without any governmental interference.

Mason and Jefferson certainly did not mean all of their words literally, that all men were created equal, and definitely not that all people (men, women, and children or people who were not of European ancestry) were created equal. Neither of the declarations meant all people or even all men. They meant members of the political nation.

Nevertheless, the two documents as adopted appeared to have made an implicit promise that applied, or could apply, or should apply, to people other than adult white men who owned property. The desires of those other people to enjoy the benefits and protections of those rights began to bring about change almost immediately. The memorable words helped animate the work of Baptists and other religious dissenters in Virginia to secure religious liberty and to separate church and state. The language expressed the ideals that drove the campaign that white men waged in the nineteenth century to secure the vote for all adult white men, not just those who owned real estate. The ideals were at the heart of the campaign to abolish slavery. And to grant the vote to freed Black men after the end of slavery. And to grant women the right to vote early in the twentieth century. And the civil rights and women's movements later in the twentieth century. Indeed, many of the most important events and changes in American history can be seen as the efforts of people to obtain and enjoy the rights and liberties that the Virginia Declaration of Rights and the Declaration of Independence appeared to promise to everybody.

Perhaps some readers may decline to allocate as profound an influence to the Virginia Declaration of Rights as to the Declaration of Independence. That would be incorrect, though, because the Declaration of Rights, which was the first of its kind in the constitutional revolution that independence set in motion in the United States, had an enormous and widespread influence. Every one of the new states that wrote a constitution during the Revolutionary era included a declaration of rights or appended a similar declaration to it. Those declarations included protections for freedom of the press, trial by jury, guarantees against forced self-incrimination, and some for freedom of religion. A careful examination of the provisions and wordings of those documents demonstrates that many of them derived directly or indirectly from the Virginia declaration. Moreover, every new state, beginning with Kentucky in 1792, also adopted a declaration, or bill, of rights. The Virginia declaration and the other state declarations also influenced the United States Bill of Rights, which Congress submitted to the states for ratification in 1789, and also the French Declaration of the Rights of Man and Citizen that same year.

Unfortunately, we have too little reliable information about how members of First Nations tribes in Virginia responded to the implied promises in the Revolutionary language of liberty. We know that they were exposed to it. At the same time, some Baptist ministers were taking the Gospel to Black Virginians, and some ministers undoubtedly worked to convert members of some of the tribes. It is one of the lamentable gaps in our understanding of the past that all Virginians share that our knowledge of the early actions and beliefs of members of First Nations tribes at that time about these important ideas remains thin.

The Revolutionary language of liberty from 1776 set off the American Revolution early in the War for Independence. The Revolutionary language of liberty would undoubtedly have been of large and lasting influence in the United States regardless of how long the war lasted or perhaps even of how it ended.

13

The Rising Sun of Religious Liberty

One of the first Virginia documents that refers explicitly to the Virginia Declaration of Rights as a guarantor of individual liberty is a petition that 160 Baptist men who lived in Prince Edward County adopted on September 24, 1776, and sent to the General Assembly. It is also one of the most eloquent and powerful of the scores of petitions on the subject of religious liberty that the General Assembly received beginning in that year. The petition is in the Records of the General Assembly, Legislative Petitions, Prince Edward County, Record Group 87, Library of Virginia.

The syntax is awkward in a few places, but run-on sentences of the sort that were common in petitions of the time need not detract from the force of the eloquent argument. The petition reads, "That we heartily approve and Chearfully submit ourselves to the form of Government adopted at your last Session"—that is, the session of the Fifth Virginia Convention of May–July, whose members, with a few changes, returned under the authority of the Virginia Constitution of 1776 to the Capitol in October 1776 as members of the first House of Delegates of the Commonwealth of Virginia.

The petitioners, "hoping that our united American States will long continue free and Independent," went on to declare, "The last Article of the Bill of Rights we also esteem as the rising Sun of religious Liberty, to releave us from a long Night of ecclesiastic Bondage: And we do most earnestly request and expect that you would go on to complete what is so nobly begun; raise religious as well as civil Liberty to the Zenith of Glory, and make Virginia an Asylum for free enquiry, knowlege, and the virtuous of every Denomination. Justice to ourselves and Posterity, as well as a regard to the honour of the Common Wealth, makes it our indispensable

Duty, in particular to intreat, That without Delay, You would pull down all Church E[s]tablishments; Abolish every Tax upon Conscience and private Judgment; and leave each Individual to rise or sink according to his Merit, and the general Laws of the Land." The petitioners concluded, "The whole amount of what we desire, is, That Our Honourable Legislature would blot out every Vestige of British Tyranny and Bondage, and define accurately between civil and ecclesiastic Authority; then leave our Lord Jesus Christ the Honour of being the Sole Lawgiver and Governor in his Church; and every one in the Things of Religion to stand or fall to Him; he being, in this respect the only rightful Master."

It was the new American language of religious liberty in the Virginia Declaration of Rights, not the old English language of religious toleration, to which the Prince Edward County Baptists appealed. They and the thousands of other Baptists, Presbyterians, Quakers, Lutherans, and others in Virginia at the time of independence worshipped under several onerous restrictions. Every Virginia taxpayer paid taxes to the Church of England to support the religious and civic responsibilities that Virginia law assigned to the church's parishes. No marriage was valid unless a minister of the Church of England celebrated it; the children of men and women who married in their own Baptist, Presbyterian, or Lutheran churches or in Quaker, Mennonite, or Church of the Brethren meetinghouses were all legally illegitimate, which imposed major problems for them. Moreover, even though the essence of the British Act of Toleration had been reenacted in Virginia in 1699, dissenters—Protestants who did not consider themselves members of the Church of England—had to apply to the royal governor for permission to erect and maintain a meetinghouse, and they could not hold meetings anywhere else, in the night, or with windows or doors closed and locked.

Dissenters had grown in number during the middle decades of the eighteenth century and considerably altered the religious culture of Virginia. In response, mobs of people, sometimes including or under the leadership of sheriffs or justices of the peace, harassed or beat Baptist ministers, broke up their religious services, or threw them in jail. In Chesterfield County, the presiding judge of the county court, Archibald Cary, who was one of the leading members of the House of Burgesses, jailed a Baptist minister. The minister nevertheless continued to preach through the window of his jail cell to members of his congregation who gathered outside. Cary reportedly erected a high wall around the jail to keep the Baptists at a distance. That was by no means the most extreme measure that officials of the colonial government took in opposition to dissenters.

Dissenters had been trying for years, without success, to obtain relief from some of the legal restrictions, but so far they had had only one small success. In August 1775, the Third Virginia Convention created a two-regiment army and adopted an ordinance that provided for paid chaplains, who in England and in the colony had always been ministers of the Church of England. The Virginia Baptist Association petitioned the convention to grant Baptist ministers "free Liberty to preach to the Troops at convenient Times without Molestation or abuse."

Patrick Henry drafted a resolution, which the convention adopted without recorded opposition, "that it be an Instruction to the Commanding Officers of the Regiments or Troops to be raised to permit dissenting Clergymen to celebrate divine Worship and to preach to the Soldiers or exhort from Time to Time as the various operations of the Military Service may admit for the ease of such scrupulous Consciences, as may not chuse to attend divine Worship as celebrated by the Chaplain."

Before the Fifth Virginia Convention began to consider the first draft for the Declaration of Rights in May 1776, forty-nine Baptists in Prince William County petitioned to be freed from some of the legal restrictions. They asked for freedom to "worship God in our own way, without interruption"; that they not be required to pay taxes to support ministers of other churches; and that marriages that dissenting ministers performed be regarded as legal. The final sentence of their petition suggests that they offered a quid pro quo: "These granted, we will gladly unite with our Brethren of other denominations, and to the utmost of our ability, promote the common cause of Freedom." The Fifth Convention referred the petition to a committee, but the committee made no recommendation before the convention adjourned on July 5, 1776.

As the wording of the petition from the Prince Edward County Baptists indicated, the promise of religious liberty that the members of the Fifth Virginia Convention inserted into the Declaration of Rights gave dissenters hope and offered them a powerful new line of argument. At every session of the General Assembly beginning in October 1776, the House of Delegates received large numbers of petitions asking for or even demanding relief from the religious and legal discrimination that the government of Virginia and the Church of England imposed on dissenters.

The petitioning was an entirely unprecedented and organized attempt to persuade the General Assembly to change the law on a fundamentally important subject. Presbyterians and some other dissenters also joined in with their own petitions. The campaign for transforming the practices of religious toleration into laws of religious freedom was the first and one of the most important consequences of, and uses of, the Revolutionary language of liberty.

Eventually, in January 1786, after more than a decade of political controversy and social ferment, the General Assembly adopted the Act for Establishing Religious Freedom, which removed all of the legal privileges that the Church of England had enjoyed, transferred its civic duties, such as caring for orphans and paupers, to local governments, and converted all religious societies into purely voluntary associations. With the possible exception of independence, that law may be the most important and revolutionary act of the entire Revolutionary period in Virginia. It must have seemed appropriate that Thomas Jefferson, who wrote the most famous phrases of the Revolutionary language of liberty, drafted the bill, and that James Madison, who had proposed the amendment to the Declaration of Rights that transformed it from a statement of religious toleration into a guarantee of religious liberty, pushed the Act for Establishing Religious Freedom through the assembly a decade later.

One choice irony is that Archibald Cary, who used his office as presiding judge of the Chesterfield County Court to jail a Baptist minister early in the 1770s, signed the Act for Establishing Religious Freedom in his capacity

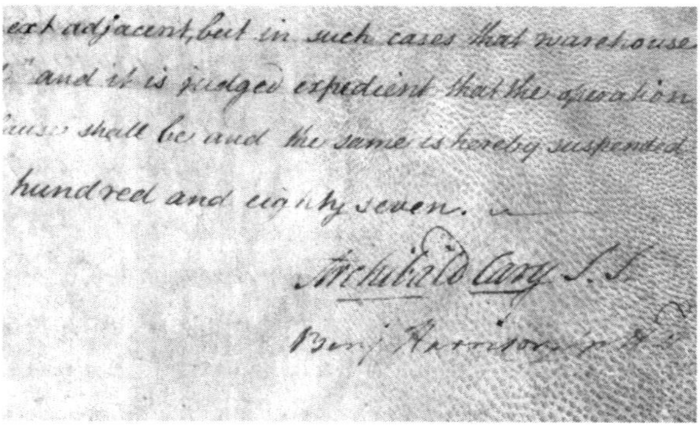
adjacent, but in such cases that warehouse
and it is judged expedient that the operation
shall be and the same is hereby suspended
hundred and eighty seven.
Archibald Cary S.S.

Detail of signatures of Benjamin Harrison, Speaker of the House of Delegates, and Archibald Cary, Speaker of the Senate of Virginia, on the 1786 Act for Establishing Religious Freedom. (Library of Virginia)

as Speaker of the Senate of Virginia. We do not know if Cary changed his mind about the dissenters or the privileged place in society and government that the Church of England had always enjoyed. He might have, or he might have signed into law a bill of which he disapproved because that was his constitutional responsibility as Speaker. Archibald Cary's signature, together with the signature of former governor Benjamin Harrison, Speaker of the House of Delegates and a signer of the Declaration of Independence, made the bill a law.

14

The Patriots

SOMETIME ABOUT 1777, ROBERT MUNFORD, a former burgess from Mecklenburg County, on the border with North Carolina, wrote a short play entitled *The Patriots.* The setting is in one of the Virginia counties and features one of the county committees that ceased to function late in 1776. We know that Munford wrote the play about 1777 or revised it in that year because it contains a brief reference to the Battle of Princeton at the beginning of January 1777. Munford had written his first play in 1770, entitled *The Candidates,* about the election of burgesses late in the colonial period. It is a short, satiric comedy that treats the foibles of people and is not, in fact, very sophisticated.

The Patriots has five acts, is in much the same style as *The Candidates,* and is not very sophisticated, either. As in *The Candidates,* the principal characters are all caricatures, as their names disclose: Meanwell and Trueman, "men of fortune" who are leading public officials in the county but unfairly suspected of being loyal to the king; committee members Thunderbolt, Squib, Colonel Strut, Summons, Brazen, and Skip, some of whom are hypocrites about politics; Mr. Tackabout, who pretends to be a Virginia patriot but is really a loyalist; Captain Flash, a recruiting officer; and Isabella, "a female politician." The play has other minor characters and several simultaneous plots, including a love affair and an exhibition of prejudice against Scotland in the persons of characters named M'Flint, M'Squeeze, and M'Gripe.

About forty years old when he wrote *The Patriots,* Munford had been educated in England, read law in Williamsburg, was a veteran of the war with France, and had represented Mecklenburg County in the House of Burgesses from 1765 to 1775. He was also the county lieutenant, the commanding officer of the militia. Munford's son published a small volume that included both of his plays and several poems in 1798, about fifteen years after he died. We have no evidence that anybody ever performed *The Patriots* during Munford's life.

It seems quite clear from *The Patriots* that Robert Munford was uneasy with the social and political ferment that accompanied the move for independence. We know from a surviving letter that he wrote in the spring of 1775 that he was already worried about the stability of the social and political systems in Virginia. In the play, members of the committee abuse some long-established local leaders and violate various social norms. Servants (enslaved people?) scheme against the interests of their masters (enslavers?); Isabella, the female politician, tries to use her political wiles to trick a man into marriage; and upstart committee members try to direct the course of public affairs in the county.

For the most part, traditional elite Virginia leaders preserved their political leadership roles during the War for Independence and the political changes that accompanied it. Potential fractures in that structure and challenges to it naturally worried men like Munford, who as a justice of the peace, former burgess, and commanding officer of the county militia stood at the top of the county's economic, social, and political hierarchies. Munford seems to express his personal ideas early in Act I when he has Trueman tell Meanwell that he has fallen in love with the daughter of Brazen, a committee member whom he describes as "a violent patriot without knowing the meaning of the word. He understands little or nothing beyond a dice-box and race-field, but thinks he knows every thing."

That kind of condescending attitude can be seen in other sources about the relationships of elite Virginia leaders and other, lesser, men during the middle decades of the eighteenth century. Because elite men believed that they deserved respect and deference and that they were entitled to play the leading roles that their social standing accorded them, they could easily be unsettled when men or women of lower standing appeared to be crossing traditional lines between the classes of white Virginians.

The elected county committee members in most Virginia counties included members of the local elite families, but more men than the small number of justices of the peace who usually manned the county courts and directed local government affairs began to take part in the management of public affairs as soon as the committees came into being during the winter of 1774–75. The character Trueman expresses his (Munford's?) dislike for the enlarged public role that Brazen and the other committee members have taken onto themselves. Munford has Trueman tell Meanwell that Brazen's "political notions are a system of perfect anarchy, but he reigns in his own family with perfect despotism," and "woe be to him that contradicts him!" As a committee man, Brazen is "fully resolved that nobody shall tyrannize over him, but very content to tyrannize over others."

Men like James Cleveland in Loudoun County and the men who signed the Lunenburg County petition that condemned the exemption of plantation overseers from military service appeared to pose a serious threat to the social and political orders. Munford saw that clearly and very likely knew about the petition from the neighboring county of Lunenburg. What Munford could not clearly foresee is that the traditional elites were largely successful during the decade after 1776 in preserving their leadership roles, even though with some limitations and adaptions on their part.

Two factors may have accounted for that. One, a very large proportion of leading public men in Virginia eventually supported independence, unlike what happened in some other colonies where the elites fractured into large groups of patriots and loyalists and took opposing sides during the war. Two, the state constitution that elite white Virginia men put into operation in the summer of 1776 explicitly limited the right to vote to the same population of men who had been able to vote since 1736—adult white males who owned at least a hundred acres of land or fifty acres of land and a house in the countryside or a lot or part of a lot in one of the two incorporated Virginia cities, Williamsburg and Norfolk. The constitution made a thoroughgoing political revolution virtually impossible.

The changes that the Revolutionary language of liberty unleashed in 1776 did not immediately reduce that political advantage for the traditional elite leaders. That advantage did not change in any fundamentally important way for seventy-five more years, until voters ratified a new state constitution in 1851. Many other changes, however, in society, in political thought, and in behavior began to work revolutionary changes that would undoubtedly have disturbed Robert Munford even more had he lived long enough to witness the consequences. He did not, and died early in 1783, a depressed and possibly alcoholic man. It is nevertheless a compliment to his insights into the society in which he benefited in almost every way that he was able early on to perceive some of the potential consequences for that society of the changes that the epoch of the American Revolution set loose.

15

Should Will Be Freed and Emancipated from Slavery?

On November 4, 1779, the House of Delegates received a petition from "Will a Negro man" that had originally been addressed "To His Excellency the Governor & Council." The petition is in the Records of the General Assembly, Legislative Petitions, King William County, Record Group 78, Library of Virginia.

The petition recites that Will "was the slave of Mrs. Ann Colvin late of the County of King William deceased who by her last will & testament in writing in consideration of the long faithful & merritorious services of your petitioner, did by her said will, direct that your petitioner for the Consideration aforesaid, should be freed and emancipated from slavery. And your petitioner being advised that he cannot take the benefit of the charitable & benevolent intentions of his said mistress in the premisses without the aid & interposition of your honorable board, humbly prays that you will take his case into consideration & grant him such releif, as to your wisdom may see meet & the justice of his case shall require—"

Before independence, enslaved Virginians could not legally become free unless they won a lawsuit for unlawful enslavement, the royal governor and Council of State proclaimed them to be free for performing some meritorious service, or by a special act of the General Assembly. Clearly, from the wording of the petition, we know that Will had received legal advice that without approval from the governor, the emancipation provision of Ann Colvin's will could not have full legal authority. That the person who drafted the petition for Will initially addressed it to the governor and Council of State suggests that the lawyer, delegate, or county clerk who drew up the document believed that the governor of the independent Commonwealth of

Virginia still had the authority that the royal governor had possessed to free enslaved people. He may have been wrong. The Constitution of 1776 specifically limited the authority of the governor of Virginia—who until June 1779 was Patrick Henry; after that, Thomas Jefferson—to take no action not specifically granted to the governor in the state constitution or in its laws, and in particular not to exercise any authority as a prerogative of office, as kings had done and as royal governors had done as the personal representatives of the king.

The governor and the Council of State received the petition on an unrecorded date. It is unclear if they thoroughly discussed the question of whether the governor of the state of Virginia still had the same authority that the royal governor of the colony had possessed to free Will. We have evidence from a later petition that they discussed whether Will deserved freedom for his meritorious service and decided that he did not.

As was the case with Baptists and other dissenters who took inspiration from the provisions of the Virginia Declaration of Rights, other Virginians and Americans took inspiration from the Revolutionary language of liberty in the Declaration of Rights and in the Declaration of Independence. Within a few years after independence, a new antislavery movement began to attract followers in the new country, including in Virginia. The most obvious contradiction between the promise of the Revolutionary language of liberty and the practices of Revolutionary Americans was the institution of slavery. Ann Colvin was not the first citizen of Virginia to try to emancipate an enslaved person during the American Revolution, nor was she the last.

During the assembly session that began in the autumn of 1779, the legislators did nothing about the petition that they had received from Will. Late in the following year, they received another petition that provided more information and that indicates that the governor and Council of State had, indeed, considered Will's claim to freedom, and that Will's white male collaborator submitted the enslaved man's original petition to the General Assembly.

"The Petition of Anne Bennet, an Infant under the Age of twenty one years, by William Alvey, her guardian," reached the House of Delegates on December 11, 1780. That petition stated that when Colvin initially wrote her will in the autumn of 1776, she bequeathed Will to two granddaughters, one of whom was the petitioner Anne Bennet, and the other of whom died soon thereafter. Colvin then made a codicil, or addendum, to her will that provided for Will to become a free man.

Bennet's petition recounted that the governor and Council of State identified no meritorious service that entitled them to emancipate Will, so his lawyer readdressed the petition to the House of Delegates. More importantly, the petition claimed that Bennet's grandmother offered freedom to Will only "On account of the fear which She Entertained of receiving Some Personal Injury from him, rather than on account of Any gratitude for his past Services, as an Evidence that this Suggestion is well founded, your Petitioner believes that She can prove, that the Slave will, after having often threatened, and once Attempted to take away his own life, in order to revenge himself on his Former Master for Giving him a Slight Correction, has made an attempt upon the life of your Petitioner's Grandmother, who was to him a most indulgent Mistress, And Constantly told her that he would never Serve any person to Whom She should Leave him. From hence it will appear, that instead of Meriting freedom, or being a proper person to become a Member of the Civil State as a free man, he Stands in Need of the watchful eye of a Master Constantly over him, to prevent him of Executing his Horrid purposes." Bennett's petition asked that Will be denied freedom.

The General Assembly did not pass a law to free Will. Whether the original will took effect and eventually freed him, anyway, is not clear. In 1782, though, the General Assembly considerably relaxed the laws concerning emancipation and allowed Virginians to free enslaved people by providing for freedom when they wrote their wills, as Ann Colvin had tried to do, or by executing a deed of manumission and registering it with the county court. By the end of the eighteenth century the population of free Black Virginians had noticeably increased. Because free women gave birth to free children, the population of free Black Virginians continued to grow after the initial burst of emancipations began to subside early in the nineteenth century.

16

Hannah Lee Corbin (Hall), Housekeeper

THE BRANCH OF THE LEE FAMILY that had its principal seat at Stratford Hall in Westmoreland County was prominent in Virginia public life from the seventeenth through the nineteenth centuries. The Revolutionary generation was especially notable. Philip Ludwell Lee, the eldest of six brothers who held important public offices, served on the Council of State from 1757 until his early death in 1774; Richard Henry Lee and Francis Lightfoot Lee both represented Virginia in the Continental Congress and signed the Declaration of Independence; Thomas Ludwell Lee served in the Virginia Convention of 1776 that adopted the Virginia Declaration of Rights and the first constitution of the new state; and Arthur Lee became an alderman of the city of London before independence, and he and William Lee served in diplomatic posts in Europe during the War for Independence.

Their sister Hannah is known to students of eighteenth-century women's history but to few other people because of a letter that one of her brothers wrote on March 17, 1778. Rather than being a leading public figure, as were her brothers, she faced serious disadvantages by being a woman and also by being a convert to the Baptist Church.

About 1747, Hannah Lee married Gawin Corbin, a member of a socially and politically prominent family. He died during the winter of 1759–60, which left her a widow with a young daughter and heir to a large estate in land and enslaved human beings. The terms of Corbin's will stipulated that if she remarried, she would have to relinquish her inheritance in land and enslaved people.

After Gawin Corbin died, Hannah Lee Corbin joined a Baptist church. Richard Lingan Hall, who had offered religious comfort to Gawin Corbin before his death, was the minister of the church. The widow and the minister fell in love and lived together, but they did not legally marry, which would have cost the widow her inheritance. They may possibly have married in the Baptist Church, but Virginia law did not recognize as legal a marriage that a minister of the Church of England did not perform. As a legally unmarried woman, even though she was living with Hall and regarded herself as married to him, she retained her inheritance. They had one son and one daughter before Hall died in 1774, and in spite of her living an unconventional life that in several respects could have been illegal, she remained on close terms with her Lee relatives.

In 1769, the daughter of Gawin Corbin and Hannah Lee Corbin took possession of part of her father's estate as his will had stipulated, but Hannah Lee Corbin (Hall) retained her own land, which exposed her to a second vulnerability because she was a woman.

Late in 1777, the General Assembly passed a law to impose new taxes on real estate with which to pay some of the expenses of the War for Independence. One provision of the law authorized "the freeholders and housekeepers of each county" to elect tax commissioners annually to assess the value of the taxable property. The word *freeholders* had appeared in Virginia election laws for more than a century by then and referred to people who owned land. The 1736 Virginia election law, which was still in force in 1777, limited the right to vote to freeholders who owned at least a hundred acres of land or fifty acres of land and a house in the country, or a house or lot in one of the two incorporated cities, Williamsburg and Norfolk. In the context of Virginia election laws and practices, the critical word *freeholders* had always had a white, male meaning.

The 1777 law, though, also allowed housekeepers to vote for tax commissioners. The law did not have so clear a meaning for the word *housekeeper*, although it had probably also been thought to mean only white men. In the eighteenth century, the word *housekeeper* signified the head of a household, possibly the owner of a house, and not, as later, a hired household manager or even cleaner. In the patriarchal society of the colonial period, men were the heads of households, even if their fathers were dead and their mothers were alive.

Hannah Lee Corbin (Hall) was a white female head of a household in 1777 when the General Assembly passed the law that required her to pay taxes on the land that she still legally owned. The following year, she apparently complained by letter to her brother Richard Henry Lee that the commissioners had overvalued her property for taxation purposes. Her letter to her brother does not survive, so we do not know precisely what she told him or asked him. Perhaps she only complained, but she may also have asked for his advice. The letter in which he replied, though it has subsequently been lost, too, was printed in an Alexandria newspaper in 1875 and then reprinted from that source early in the twentieth century, in James Curtis Ballagh, ed., *The Letters of Richard Henry Lee,* 2 vols. (New York, 1911–14), 1:392–94.

From the text of Lee's reply to his sister, we know that he believed that as a housekeeper she had "as legal a right to vote as any other person" in the annual elections of county tax commissioners. His letter has sometimes been mistakenly construed to indicate that Hannah Lee Corbin (Hall) asked for the right to vote and that her brother agreed, but in fact all that his letter clearly indicates is that he informed his sister that, in his opinion, she could vote for tax commissioners. Whether either of them ever believed that she gained or should have gained the right to vote for members of the General Assembly, the only other elected public officials in the 1770s, is not clear but probably unlikely from the wording of his letter.

No researcher has discovered any evidence that any Virginia women voted for tax commissioners while the 1777 law was in force or tried to vote for any members of the legislature. In fact, the General Assembly revised the tax law in 1781 and empowered the county courts, not freeholders and housekeepers, to select tax commissioners.

Another episode in the next decade is also susceptible to more than one interpretation. In 1787, Ann Makemie Holden, of Accomack County, on the Eastern Shore, the peninsula between Chesapeake Bay and the Atlantic Ocean, deeded land to four male relatives who did not then own real estate. In the deeds, Holden required that the men "Vote at the Annual Elections for the most Wise and Discreet men who have proved themselves real friends to the American Independence to represent the County of Accomack" in the General Assembly. Holden died not long after she executed the deeds, and it is not clear from her words, as it might have become from her actions, whether she merely enfranchised four male relatives or hoped through them to have four proxy votes in elections for members of the General Assembly. Nor is it clear whether her requirement for how they would vote was a conditional one that would allow her or her heirs to recover the land if the men did not vote for the men she would have favored, if that could be reliably ascertained.

Women, both white and Black, gained little or nothing from the American Revolution, in spite of the strong appeal of the Revolutionary language of liberty. The opposition to slavery that grew out of the Language of Liberty—equality and the rights to life, liberty, and the pursuit of happiness—eventually brought freedom to some enslaved women, but during the early years of the nineteenth century, white women, both elite and non-elite women, labored in their households for the benefit of their families and in the shadows of the men in their families.

We know from a very small number of scattered records that in three or four instances in the nineteenth century and early in the twentieth, a few Virginia women who owned property participated in local referenda on taxes or whether to put into effect in their towns an optional state law that mandated residential racial segregation; but the state's constitutions expressly limited the right to vote for public officials to men in 1776, 1830, 1851, 1864, 1869, and 1902. Virginia women never had the opportunity or the right to vote for candidates for any office until ratification of the Nineteenth Amendment to the Constitution of the United States in August 1920.

17

Lynch's Law

Beginning at the time of the war between Great Britain and France in the 1750s and 1760s, which most Americans called the French and Indian War and everybody else in the English-speaking world called the Seven Years' War, the government of Virginia owned and operated a lead mine in the part of southwestern Virginia that became Montgomery County in 1776 and Wythe County in 1789. The lead that men extracted and smelted there provided metal for bullets and cannonballs in the last major war of the colonial period and in the War for Independence. The labor force during the War for Independence consisted of white Virginia men, including some experienced white miners originally from Wales, some white criminals who were sentenced to labor there, hired enslaved workers, and other enslaved men whom the government had confiscated from suspected loyalists and sent to the mine to work.

Colonel Charles Lynch, the man who had reported John Hook to the Bedford County Committee in 1775, was one of the militia officers assigned to run and protect the mine in 1780. The other militia officers included Robert Adams, James Callaway, and William Preston, all of them prominent men in south-central and southwestern Virginia. In the summer of 1780, the officers believed that they had good reason to fear that loyalists in the region, spurred on by English agents, members of some First Nations tribes that the English agents may have enlisted, and enslaved people, might combine forces to capture or destroy the mine.

The officers took preventive action before the situation became dangerous or got out of hand. They conducted no formal trials to ascertain guilt but nevertheless punished some of the suspected men at the whipping post, forced some of their followers into the American army, extracted oaths of allegiance from others under duress, and in one or more instances looked aside as frightened or angry local men plundered the property of suspected loyalists. The mob violence that the officers condoned and their own participation as leaders in violently putting down the suspected uprising is almost certainly the event that led to the phrase "lynch law" and inspired the verb *lynch*. The phrase and word initially indicated only extralegal mob violence and did not necessarily imply that any of the victims died or that anybody was hanged, which is what the terms came to imply a century later when lynching became a too-common form of violence that white supremacists employed to terrorize or punish Black people.

Charles Lynch, so far as we know, took no credit for coining the phrase, but a letter dated May 1, 1782, and that appears to be in Lynch's atrocious handwriting, described another incident and characterized it with the phrase "Lynch,s Law." The letter survives in the Executive Papers of Governor Benjamin Harrison, Record Group 3, Library of Virginia, because the recipient conveyed it to another man, who in turn gave it to the governor. Lynch's use of the phrase suggests that within two years of the punishment of the suspected loyalists, it may have come into local or regional use. He did not bother to explain what he meant when he wrote the words, nor did the other men who read the letter apparently ask about its meaning. They knew.

Two footnotes: On December 24, 1782, the General Assembly passed a special law that specifically named Charles Lynch and the other three officers and retroactively legalized their violent actions. The exigencies and emergencies of warfare too often produce dangers and retaliations that in peacetime would be handled very differently, and that sometimes, as at the lead mine in 1780, result in violent and unjust behavior. In this instance, undoubtedly because of the importance of the mine to the conduct of the war, the General Assembly gave its approval to an act of mob violence and excused its leaders.

A seventy-five-foot shot tower was erected near the mine on the New River early in the nineteenth century to produce lead shot. Smelting and producing shot there evidently ceased before being revived during the American Civil War. The tower is now a National Historical Landmark and the site of a small Virginia state park.

18

Inferior Militia Officers

DURING THE WAR FOR INDEPENDENCE, regiments of Continental Army units served from every state and in every state. Every state also had companies or regiments of militia, citizen soldiers who trained from time to time and often, but not always, served on active duty in the field alongside regular army units. At the beginning of the war, members of the militia regarded themselves, and their fellow citizens regarded them, as the best line of defense against tyranny. The militia had a very long history in England and also in the colonies, where, when the War for Independence began, people generally regarded the militia as the natural counterweight to the power of despotic kings and their hired, professional armies.

In Virginia, militia companies took part in defense of the frontier when members of First Nations tribes threatened and sometimes mustered when rumors of uprisings of enslaved people swept through the countryside. The most famous Virginia militiaman of all, George Washington, wore his militia colonel's uniform when he represented Virginia at the Second Continental Congress, which in June 1775 appointed him a general and commander in chief of the Continental Army.

On several occasions, Virginia militiamen lived up to the hopes of their fellow citizens. Virginia militiamen under the command of General William Campbell fought alongside militiamen from other states and won a critical battle of the War for Independence at King's Mountain, South Carolina, in October 1780. On the whole, however, militia companies were often ill-prepared for action and ill-equipped, as well; and they often served in the field only for brief periods of time. Rotation of militia units in and out of active service necessarily meant that few militiamen were engaged in the service long enough to become valuable soldiers. General Washington, himself, lost faith in the militia and during the war advocated recruitment of regular army soldiers rather than continued reliance on the militia.

In the summer of 1780, Governor Thomas Jefferson ordered that General Edward Stevens march several companies of Virginia militia, about 700 men, south to reinforce regular Continental Army units under the command of General Horatio Gates to prevent a British force in South Carolina from marching north through the Carolinas toward Virginia. Stevens had experience in the field. As a lieutenant colonel in the Culpeper Minutemen, he had pursued British and loyalist volunteers who attacked the Great Bridge in December 1775. In 1780, Stevens and his Virginia militiamen, along with militia companies from North Carolina and several regiments of Continental Army soldiers from Maryland and Delaware, faced a large force under the command of General Charles, Lord Cornwallis, which had captured Charleston, South Carolina, in May.

At about 10 p.m. on August 15, General Gates ordered that his combined force begin a long night march toward the British, who were then near Camden, South Carolina. His entire force had never maneuvered together, and many of the militiamen had no battlefield experience and no training working in tandem with other units. Gates then erred by assigning the untested Virginia militia to defend the left flank, which meant that they faced the best of the experienced British soldiers.

The two armies fought a pitched battle just north of Camden on August 16. The Americans outnumbered the British by more than two to one, but many of the inexperienced Virginia militiamen were poorly equipped and poorly trained. Several companies of militiamen panicked, threw down their guns, and fled at the first sounds of gunfire. The battle was an embarrassing defeat for the Americans, who suffered casualties later estimated at about 50 percent, compared to British casualties of about 15 percent.

When Washington learned of the defeat, he replaced Gates as commander in the southern theater with Nathanael Greene, one of the best and most successful American generals. The debacle at Camden allowed the British to march through the Carolinas and eventually into Virginia, where they plundered and rampaged with minimal resistance well into 1781.

On November 19, 1780, the House of Delegates received a long petition from a company of militiamen in Amherst County, between Charlottesville and Lynchburg. They had been present at Camden and were deeply embarrassed at their conduct in fleeing from the British rather than fighting them. By petitioning the General Assembly the militiamen sought to explain their behavior and to earn a chance to recover their reputations by volunteering to take the field again. The petition is preserved in the Records of the General Assembly, Legislative Petitions, Amherst County, Record Group 78, Library of Virginia.

The militiamen from Amherst County blamed the commanding officers of their company for their own disgraceful conduct at Camden. By law, county courts selected militia officers. Many young officers had no military backgrounds and received their commissions because they were members of elite, local families. For example, before the War for Independence, Thomas Jefferson, who had absolutely no military training or ambitions, was the county lieutenant of Albemarle County, the commanding officer with the rank of senior colonel in the county. The appointment was a result of his social and economic standing, not his military training or experience. That was commonplace throughout the officer corps of Virginia militia.

Virginia law had for decades required militia companies to meet periodically to drill and train, but officers and men sometimes failed to attend, and the events were as much or more social occasions than proper musters to prepare men to act together to defend themselves and their families. Even during the war, few people apparently undertook to provide the militia with adequate training, equipment, or properly qualified leadership.

The petition from the Amherst County militiamen blamed their incompetent and amateur gentlemen officers for the men's "being wholly unacquainted with Military Discipline, which we had not time to learn." Had the county militia been under proper direction, the men should have learned military discipline at musters and how to maneuver in the field. Moreover, the men complained, they were "Greatly Exhausted by Fatigue at that hot Season, which we had not been inured to; Dispirited for want of Rest & Diet"—adequate rations—"and Panick-struck by the Noise and Terror of a Battle which was entirely New to most of us." They also maintained that "had our inferior Militia Officers been experienc'd in Military

Discipline or Capable of encouraging us by their Example as well as Orders and particularly had we not been drawn up in such Close Order but had more space to Act; And Lastly been Permitted to Fire on the Enemy before we receiv'd their Fire, or before we came so near We verily believe the Event"—their behavior and therefore the outcome of the battle—would have been "Otherwise." By the common phrase "inferior Militia Officers," the militiamen meant officers of lower rank, company-grade officers, not field-grade officers, major and above; but the words also clearly suggested inferior in quality.

The petitioners concluded by requesting a respite from militia service in the field to care for their families and that regular, experienced army officers be appointed to command them. Under those circumstances, they promised to be ready to return to the field, "That we shall by our future Conduct not only retrieve our own Reputation as Citizens of a Free State But also the losses & Dishonour which our Country has Sustain'd by our former Pusillanimity." The General Assembly did not grant them the relief or the second chance that they requested.

In 1781, the militia failed again when a British column occupied the new capital city of Richmond and marched all the way to Charlottesville, where the General Assembly had fled on the approach of the British. The British captured several members of the legislature, including Daniel Boone, who was a member of the House of Delegates at the time, and almost captured Governor Thomas Jefferson, who escaped by galloping his horse over a mountain as the British approached Monticello.

One consequence of the ability of the British to maneuver without much effective opposition in Virginia was the destruction of most of the executive and legislative archive of the colony at the time of the British occupation of Richmond. Copies of many of the executive and legislative records survived in London, but for the most part students of Virginia history did not have access to the bulk of those historic documents until the second half of the twentieth century.

In 1784, after the war, when Patrick Henry, a former governor and also commander in chief of the Virginia forces in the winter of 1775–76, was governor again, he urged the General Assembly to reform the militia. The law that the assembly enacted increased the authority of the governor to appoint and displace officers with the hope that in the future the militia would have better, more experienced leadership and be better trained. Members of county courts, though, which appointed militia officers, defeated the reform by obstructing implementation of the new law in what can be accurately described as a mass act of passive-aggressive noncompliance.

19

James, a Spy

THE LAST MILITARY ACTION of the War for Independence in Virginia culminated in the surrender of the British army under the command of General Charles, Lord Cornwallis, at Yorktown on October 19, 1781. Most Virginians at the time considered the surrender as the end of the war, and many Americans now regard it as the end of the American Revolution; but much unfinished business remained, including the working out of the implications of the Revolutionary language of liberty from 1776 and the incompatibility that many people of the time perceived between the institution of slavery and the establishment of a new democratic republic based on the consent of the governed.

Several thousand Virginians escaped slavery during the war, even though many of them died trying to reach freedom under the protection of the British. During the early years of the war, General George Washington and the Continental Congress resisted taking volunteer free or enslaved Black men into the army. Eventually, however, several units of Black soldiers served in the army, and other Black men rendered other services during the war. Some of the Virginians received their freedom for their military service.

None of them is more celebrated in Virginia than the man who when he petitioned the General Assembly in November 1786 identified himself as "James (a slave belonging to Will: Armistead of New Kent county)." He is often and incorrectly identified as James Armistead, but he never used the surname of his enslaver, so far as we know, and the petition includes no surname for him at all. The petition is in the Records of the General Assembly, Legislative Petitions, New Kent County, Record Group 78, Library of Virginia. It was actually the second petition that James submitted. His first petition reached the assembly in 1784 shortly before the session adjourned, and the legislators did not have time to consider it or act on it. The second petition was successful.

James was about thirty-three years old when the British invaded Virginia in 1781. His enslaver, William Armistead, was then a state commissary of military supplies, which may help explain how James came to be engaged in military espionage. In the petition and in his own words, he recited that he was "perswaded of the just right which all mankind have to Freedom, notwithstanding his own state of bondage, with an honest desire to serve his Country in its defence thereof."

James related that in 1781, "during the ravages of Lord Cornwallis thro' this state," he had obtained "the permission of his Master" to "enter into the service" of the Marquis de Lafayette, the young French general who had temporary command of the combined French and Continental forces in the state. In the guise of a servant, a teamster (driver of a team of horses and a wagon), or perhaps a common laborer, James could move between the military lines easier and attract less attention to himself than a white man could.

"That during the time of his serving the Marquiss," James's petition continued, "he often at the peril of his life found means to frequent the British Camp; by which means he kept open a channel of the most useful communications to the army of the state: That at the different times your petitioner conveyed inclosures, from the Marquiss into the Enemies lines, of the most secret & important kind; the possession of which if discovered on him would have most certainly endangered the life of your petitioner: That he undertook & performed all commands with chearfulness & fidelity, in Opposition to the persuasion & example of many thousands of his unfortunate condition. For proof of the above your petitioner begs leave to refer to certificate of the Marquiss Lafeyette hereto annexed; & after taking his case as here stated into consideration, he humbly intreats that he may be granted that Freedom, which he flatters himself he has in some degree contributed to establish; & which he hopes always to prove himself worthy of."

James concluded his petition with a remarkable request. He stated that he did not "desire even this inestimable favor, unless his present master from whom he has experienced every thing which can make tolerable the state of slavery, shall be made adequate compensation for the loss of a valuable workman."

General Lafayette endorsed the plea of the petition in the "certificate" that James included with it. The valuable pieces of information that James brought to him, Lafayette explained, "from the Ennemy's Camp were Industriously Collected and Most faithfully deliver'd. He perfectly Acquitted Himself with some Important Commissions I Gave Him and Appears to me Entitled to Every Reward his Situation Can Admit of."

Early in 1787, the General Assembly passed a law to grant James his freedom from slavery for his meritorious wartime service to Virginia. He then took the surname Lafayette and was known thereafter as James Lafayette. A portrait of General Lafayette that the French artist Jean-Baptiste Le Paon painted in 1785 depicts the general at Yorktown with a Black man, presumably James, standing at his side but dressed implausibly in the livery of a French serving man. James was a spy, not a mere servant.

James Lafayette returned to New Kent County following the end of the war. Long after he gained his freedom, he purchased a small farm there in 1816. Two years later, he successfully applied for a military pension. The General Assembly granted him $60 and allowed him annually to collect from the state treasury an additional $40.

James Lafayette was apparently pretty well known for a Black man, perhaps because he went into the capital city twice a year to collect his pension, and he owned a small amount of land. A report in a Richmond newspaper in 1824 described him as "a very venerable and respectable free black man." By that time he was one of only a small number of Virginians who could

James Lafayette (ca. 1748–1830), engraving after a painting by John B. Martin, ca. 1824. (Visual Studies Collection, Library of Virginia)

still boast a personal relationship with the Marquis de Lafayette. In the autumn of that year, James Lafayette traveled to Richmond when the famous Frenchman visited the city at the beginning of his triumphant tour of the United States. The aged general spotted his namesake in the crowd and reportedly called to him by name and embraced him. The artist John Blennerhasset Martin painted a portrait of James Lafayette about that time, one of the few portraits from life that we have of a Black veteran of the War for Independence. James Lafayette died, probably at his New Kent County home, on August 9, 1830.

20

Continental Army Veterans

JAMES LAFAYETTE WAS VERY FORTUNATE. As a result of his contributions to the outcome of the War for Independence, he gained his personal freedom and lived to become a minor celebrity and an owner of real estate. He also lived a long and apparently fruitful life. Army officers who emerged from the war in good health usually did well, also. In 1779, the General Assembly offered half-pay for life as an incentive to officers who agreed to serve until the end of the war. Congress also offered officers half-pay for life but in 1783 changed that to a lump-sum payment equal to five years' full pay. Common soldiers, however, were not so fortunate. The government of Virginia offered various kinds of bounties to encourage enlistment, but the state initially offered no pension or relief benefits at all, except in individual instances such as James Lafayette's, who applied directly to the General Assembly for special treatment. The assembly offered half-pay for seven years to the survivors of enlisted men who died or were killed in the service of the United States but nothing to veterans. The federal government did not do anything for common soldiers until 1818 and then only for veterans who were in serious need of financial assistance.

Applications for federal pensions filed in accordance with the 1818 act of Congress are preserved as part of Record Group 15 in the National Archives and Records Administration, in Washington, D.C. Some of them contain detailed accounts of soldiers' experiences during the war and are a valuable resource for understanding those experiences. In a very unusual instance in Virginia, perhaps a unique one, the county clerk in Frederick County entered into the public records of the county the affidavits that several local men filed in the summer and autumn of 1820 to document the needy status of veterans so as to qualify under the law of 1818. The county clerk recorded their affidavits on page 439 of the Frederick County Order Book (1817–20), and on pages 2, 8, and 41–42 in the Frederick County Minute Book (1820–22).

Henry Harris, aged sixty-six, stated on August 1, 1820, that for five years he had served in Continental cavalry units recruited in Virginia. "My occupation" in 1820, he explained, "is that of doing little jobs of laying hearths plaistering and white washing and I am in pretty good health but not able to do much at hard labor I have a wife of the Same age as myself who is very decreped, and is unable to do any thing of consequence And I have one daughter living with me who is about twenty four years of age who assists us in the family and works herself at spinning but can contribute nothing of consequence for our aid." Harris owned no real estate, and his personal property then consisted of "One table four chairs one pot, one Dutch oven, one skillit 6 plates one Coffee urn six cups and Saucers Six Knives and forks three dishes one chest, one Spinning Wheel, two trowels two white wash brushes and one Stone trimmer." The court estimated that the total value of his property was $10.

Two days later, George Wright, aged fifty-seven years, made his mark on an affidavit, which suggests that he was illiterate or physically no longer able to write his name. The document recorded that he had served in a different Virginia cavalry regiment than Henry Harris. Wright swore that he did not have "any property or securities contracts or debts due to me" or any regular income other than what he earned doing farm work as a day laborer. "I have a lame arm and back by which I am Often laid up I have no family but a daughter who lives with me, she is twenty two years of age and keeps House for me." Wright owned "a tract of land in the Allegainy Mountains of two hundred acres," which he may have received as an enlistment bonus, but "it brings me in nothing nor can I sell it for anything, it is indeed of no value." His personal property consisted of "Two rough Tables, one Cupboard, a small chest three Chairs two sheats, Six plates, Six Knives and forks, one small pan one Small pot, one griddle, one Skillet, some old barrels and five pewter Spoons." The court valued Wright's personal property at $50.

The same day that George Wright made his mark at the courthouse, sixty-three-year-old Christopher Bendinger also made his mark on an affidavit. A veteran of a Pennsylvania company of riflemen during the war, he was then a farmer in Frederick County and had probably done day labor, like

Wright. Bendinger owned no land, "nor am I able to work being disabled in one of my arms—I have a wife about Sixty years of age who is infirm and not able to do much and four daughters living with me the oldest is about twenty five years of age and the youngest ten or eleven they assist their mother a little about House work and work for themselves most part of the time." Bendinger owned "One small house, two Cows, one Sow and pigs, one Stack of hay containing about a ton and a quarter half a dozen old chairs two tables, one pot; one dutch oven, one chest, one small old corner cupboard a few plates and Knives and forks," altogether worth $60.

In November 1820, Isaac Payne, also aged sixty-three, signed his affidavit at the courthouse in Winchester. He declared that after he served three years in a Connecticut infantry regiment, he paid a substitute in April 1780 to serve the remainder of his term of enlistment; then from September 1781 until he was discharged in December 1783, he served in a Massachusetts regiment. During the war, Payne "was in several Skirmishes but no general battle." He did not indicate why or when he moved to Frederick County, Virginia, where he worked as a tailor in 1820. He then had "a wife aged twenty five years, who is very sickly and hardly able to do House work and a son three years old and a daughter one year old." Payne owned "One old Walnut table, three split bottom chairs, one small pine chest, one Iron Tea Kettle, one iron Skillet, one new brass Candle stick, one pair of Scissors one pen Knife and one flour band." He did not indicate what the "flour band" was, but it is possible that the clerk who recorded the document misunderstood what Payne had said or so muddled the spelling that the meaning is now unclear. The court valued his whole property at $7.50.

The poor Frederick County veterans who recorded their economic need in 1820 did so in language that the county clerk may have significantly influenced, especially in the cases of the men who were unable to sign their names. The language obscures the personal feelings of the applicants and their family members. One wonders whether, if they had known about the objections that James Cleveland had made in neighboring Loudoun County early in 1776 about the distinctions between the pay of officers and enlisted men, any of these men or members of their families regretted the years of dangerous military service for which, other than political independence from Great Britain and whatever personal pride they may have enjoyed as a result, they received very little reward.

Except in the instance of Christopher Bendinger, who owned a small house, none of the men owned any land in the county (George Wright owned some land elsewhere), so according to the state constitution they were not able to vote, which denied them the right to participate in their own government, which is what Revolutionary leaders insisted was the purpose of securing independence.

From these men's statements of need, unlike in the full files of applications in the National Archives, we gain no sense of the legacy that their service and their long lives toiling to make a living left them. From these brief affidavits in the records of Frederick County, we learn some things about their lives in old age. Did they resent being less well-off and less well provided for than the officers? Did they regard themselves as more or less fortunate than other men who may not have served but who also lived long lives of hard work? Did it require some special desperation to have to go to the courthouse to document their need in public? What did they think about their lives and especially about their participation in what was the most important public event of their time, the War for Independence? What, if anything, did their friends and neighbors think about the veterans in their midst and their needy circumstances?

Historians and some public men with political agendas then and later debated what the legacies of the American Revolution were and who was entitled to credit for which achievements or blame for which setbacks. What most men and women who lived through the events thought about those issues is much more difficult to recover. Were they proud of what they had done? Did they eventually forget the details of their service? Did many of them suffer from what was later called post-traumatic stress disorder?

Thinking more broadly, one wonders about the many thousands of other old or infirm Virginians who had few or no economic resources. Most old people generally—and being sixty years of age or older and having worked all your life, as the veterans had done, meant that you were old—were in some degree of need. Perhaps some of them were able to rely on family members who could provide assistance. Nobody then received a pension from working in an office or in a factory or for laboring on a farm, and no such things as Social Security, Medicare, or the welfare state enabled needy elderly people to ease their personal circumstances. It may have been the common lot of old men and women then that they were not self-sufficient.

21

The Great Scarcity of Money

THE EXECUTIVE PAPERS OF Governor Benjamin Harrison, Record Group 3, Library of Virginia, contains a letter dated March 20, 1782, that Samuel Brown and seven other men in Greenbrier County sent to Thomas Adams with a request that Adams assist them. Greenbrier County was one of several new counties that the General Assembly had created after independence that were west of the Blue Ridge and Allegheny Mountains. Greenbrier and its county seat, Lewisburg, became part of the state of West Virginia in 1863.

Why the men enlisted the assistance of Thomas Adams is not quite clear. Perhaps their own elected senators and delegates in the General Assembly had not adequately helped them obtain their objectives. In selecting Adams, they appear to have made a wise choice. A native Virginian, he had been an influential merchant in and around Richmond before he moved to London in 1762, where for a decade he engaged in trade between England and Virginia. Adams returned to Virginia and was a businessman of importance in Richmond during the War for Independence and one of the major property owners in the state. The General Assembly appointed him a Virginia delegate to the Continental Congress in 1778, but he resigned for personal reasons the following year.

Adams owned a large amount of western land, which he probably acquired speculatively, in hopes of selling it for a profit to some of the families that moved to the west. Adams, himself, also moved west, but not all the way to Greenbrier County. One year after he received the men's letter and gave it to Governor Harrison, a signer of the Declaration of Independence, Adams won election to the Senate of Virginia from the district that included the counties of Shenandoah, Rockingham, Rockbridge, and Augusta, east and northeast of Greenbrier County.

The men who signed the letter to Adams complained about the work of several commissioners whom the General Assembly had appointed to adjust, or rectify, competing land claims that several decades of haphazard surveying had created. In the decades before the War for Independence, land speculators like Adams as well as individual settlers had hired surveyors to assist them in obtaining grants, also called patents, to land that no other white men had legally claimed under Virginia law. The speculators, surveyors, and settlers completely ignored the claims of members of First Nations tribes who had occupied and used the land for many centuries. The white men designated the land as waste, vacant, or unseated.

The men who wrote to Adams charged that speculators or well-to-do settlers had hired lawyers to press their claims with the commissioners, which left people who did not have good legal representation, such as themselves, at a disadvantage. Furthermore, they believed that some of the commissioners or their lawyers harbored "Designs to favour their own purposes," perhaps because "the Doubtfull party" almost always selected one particular lawyer, who almost always succeeded in obtaining what he and his clients desired.

The result, Adams's correspondents reported, was that their money had been "artfuly Grappled away." From "the great scarsity of money," they could not hire their own lawyers. They concluded, "wee shall ever acknowledge it the most Greatful favour if you'd Remonstrate to the Governor in our Behalf" and assist them in having new commissioners appointed who understood the problems of western men and were not at the same time interested parties in settling claims to some of the same land.

For many years, competing claims, inadequate survey records, and many other factors complicated the lives of men and women who claimed ownership of western lands. Even after Adams presented the letter to the governor, the government of Virginia did little to relieve the western settlers and resolve the competing claims. In any event, it would almost certainly have required legislative intervention to sort out the confusion. The problems persisted for decades. The first constitution of Kentucky, in 1792, and even so late as the first constitution of West Virginia, in 1863, contained specific provisions to assist residents secure uncontested deeds to the land that in some instances had been in their families for decades or that recent purchasers believed were vulnerable to legal challenge under the doubts that the old Virginia laws and practices had created.

In the short term, "the great scarsity of money" also created many other problems. Without sufficient money, either coins or paper currency, western men and women had difficulty purchasing supplies or engaging in small-scale commerce with their neighbors. They no doubt carried on some of their local business affairs by barter or buying and selling in kind or on credit. Lacking the ability in their then-remote mountain places of residence to produce large cash crops on their land, they did not have opportunities, even after the end of the war reopened commerce with England, to establish long-term commercial relationships with mercantile firms in the east or on the coast to which they could sell what they produced or from which they could buy what they needed.

And perhaps worst of all, "the great scarsity of money" jeopardized their futures when tax collectors showed up. Virginia tax laws usually required payment in money and with a few exceptions did not, despite repeated recommendations from westerners, allow payment in kind. Occasionally during the war, the General Assembly had permitted some such public obligations to be discharged in kind by providing animals or forage or grain for the army and its horses; but by usually requiring payment in money, the state government imposed very difficult conditions on people who had access to very little. Throughout the backcountry, as the settlements west of the crests of the eastern mountains are called, in Virginia and in other states, the inability of people to pay their taxes produced widespread hardship and anger between the war and the end of the century.

Indeed, two years after the men signed their letter to Thomas Adams, Andrew Donnally, the sheriff of Greenbrier County, petitioned the General Assembly because he was in legal trouble for not paying into the state treasury the tax revenue that it was his legal duty to collect. He explained that "notwithstanding the utmost exercions of himself and Deputies" they were "from the Scarcity of cash Unable to Collect the same." They took legal action against some delinquent taxpayers to seize some of their property in lieu of paying the taxes; however, although "Divers sales of Delinquants effects were proposed, but not a Single article could be sold." Some potential purchasers were probably in the same condition as the delinquent taxpayers who labored under the difficulties of the scarcity of cash. Or perhaps they refused to buy out of sympathy with their neighbors.

The sheriff also complained that he received "some paper Money Issued under the resolutions of Congress . . . but upon offering the same in payment at the Treasury with the Specie I have received"—specie was gold or silver coins—"it was refused." Unable to transport by road some "Commutables," or payments in kind that he received and that some tax laws allowed people to use in lieu of money, he lost about £300. The sheriff therefore asked that the General Assembly, "from The impossibility in the present Circumstances of things, that they will grant him such farther respite of Time to pay in the ballance due to the publick as they should Judge reasonable; and also Exonerate him from the payment of the Ten per Centum charged on the amount of the Execution Issued against him" as a penalty.

The outcome of the sheriff's request is not easy to ascertain; nor is it entirely clear whether, as we would reasonably expect, other county sheriffs in the west, who collected all state and local taxes, were in the same bind as Donnally was in Greenbrier County. What is quite clear, though, is that at the end of the War for Independence, with the westward migration increasing, hardships for the people who moved to the west sometimes appeared to be as difficult to surmount as the Alleghenies themselves.

That made it hard for entrepreneurs who raised corn and converted it into whiskey, a good cash crop, to develop transportation networks in the mountains to take their goods to market in the east or to accumulate cash with which to establish small manufacturing enterprises. Consequently, the economic development of the mountain areas of western Virginia proceeded more slowly than elsewhere.

One more thing is sometimes visible in postwar petitions, especially from western parts of Virginia. To an extent, the formal, deferential tone of documents that western men sent to government officials in Richmond began to change. "In this Address," some men began when they asked the General Assembly in 1785 to create a new western state out of the Kentucky region of Virginia, "we have discarded the complimentary Stile of adulation & insincerity—it becomes Freemen when speaking to Fr[eemen], to imploy the plain, man[ly] Lan[gu]age of Independence." By that, they evidently meant personal independence, the democratic privilege that western Virginians had been asserting for many years and that by the end of the War for Independence had become more prevalent in the west. (The letters enclosed within the square brackets replace characters missing from the frayed last line on a page of the petition.)

22

The Inheritance of Catherine McCall

THE PETITION THAT ELIZABETH FLOOD, of Essex County, prepared and submitted to the General Assembly on May 18, 1782, on behalf of her granddaughter, Catherine McCall, contains one of the longest and most detailed records of members of a family whom the War for Independence separated and of the emotional hardships that the separation produced. The petition is filed in the Records of the General Assembly, Legislative Petitions, Essex County, Record Group 78, Library of Virginia.

In 1782, Elizabeth Flood was the widow of a prosperous medical doctor and was also the mother-in-law of Archibald McCall, who before the war had been a partner in the firm of John McCall & Company, a Glasgow, Scotland, trading company that exported manufactured goods to America and imported Virginia-grown tobacco to Great Britain. He had conducted his business in the Essex County port town of Tappahannock. He also had other local business partners, including his cousin George McCall, and he sometimes transacted his business with another Virginia partner as McCall & Shedden. During the years that Archibald McCall resided in Essex County, he prospered, married Elizabeth Flood's daughter, and had two daughters. Widowed, McCall sent his very young daughters to Scotland in 1773 "to give them an Education which might add dignity to their fortune."

McCall came under suspicion as a loyalist when the disputes between the colonies and the British government turned violent because in the autumn of 1775, he traveled to Norfolk and appeared to have joined the royal governor, John Murray, fourth Earl of Dunmore, at his headquarters there. As is apparent from the petition of Elizabeth Flood and also from the surviving exchange of letters between Archibald and George McCall, he was on his way to Scotland to be with his little girls.

"Their fate is a convincing proof," Elizabeth Flood's petition stated in a transparent attempt to gain maximum sympathy from the members of the legislature, "that all human projects for the attainment of felicity, are but visionary dreams, that the ways of Providence are too intricate to be traced by our weak understandings, and that we are permited at some times, to rise to the highest pinacle of hope, only that we may be plunged with the greater certainty into the black Abyss of dispair! Your Petitioner Elizabeth has lived to see the manly, liberal, paternal conduct of her son in Law, imputed to him as a crime, and by Law made punishable with the confiscation of his estate."

As a consequence of Archibald McCall's being charged as a loyalist for leaving Virginia a few months before independence, the state government did indeed confiscate his property. In the meantime, he (and Elizabeth Flood) also had to endure the death of the elder of his daughters (Elizabeth's granddaughter). The younger daughter, Flood informed the legislators, was then "at the age of Puberty"—it is very remarkable that she mentioned puberty at all—and ought to be with her grandmother in Virginia because the girl had no such close female relatives in Great Britain.

When Elizabeth Flood prepared her petition, Archibald McCall had expressed "his earnest desire to return" to Virginia "with his Daughter, and become a citizen thereof." The war had prevented him and his daughter from returning to Virginia, where she could claim her inheritance from her maternal grandfather. Elizabeth Flood enlisted George McCall to help prepare the petition to the General Assembly "to implore its generous interposition to ward off the destruction and ruin, which hangs over Archibald McCall and his daughter, and the consequent reduction of the Gray hairs of your petitioner Elizabeth with sorrow to the Grave.—They therefore most humbly intreat this honourable house, to exercise its Clemency, the best and most darling attribute of Heaven."

Separations of families in wartime are always traumatic, and in the case of the War for Independence, too numerous to catalog. Some Virginia families who were much more prominent and influential than the Flood and McCall families were divided politically as well as geographically. In 1775, when Archibald McCall left Tappahannock, the attorney general of the colony, John Randolph, had just left his native Virginia to take his wife and daughters to

England. He remained loyal to his king even though his brother, Peyton Randolph, the last Speaker of the House of Burgesses, who died shortly after he left, had taken the other side and was the first president of the Continental Congress. John Randolph's son, Edmund Randolph, sided with the colonists, too, and had already left home in Williamsburg to serve on General George Washington's staff.

The famous and wealthy, but badly in debt, Byrd family was also divided. In 1775, the third William Byrd held a lifetime royal appointment to the Council of State, which made him an influential executive advisor to the governor, a member of the upper House of the General Assembly, and a judge of the General Court, the highest court in the colony. He disapproved of the protests that Virginians and other Americans made during the years before independence. One of his sons served in the British army during the War for Independence, but another resigned his position as an ensign in the British navy and along with Edmund Randolph served on the staff of General Washington. In November 1775, when Governor Dunmore issued a proclamation that offered freedom to servants and enslaved Virginians who left their masters and mistresses to fight against them and for the king, William Byrd changed his mind and offered his experience as a colonel of the Second Virginia Regiment during the Seven Years' (or French and Indian) War. But Congress turned him down, probably at the recommendation of the Virginia delegates. He committed suicide at the beginning of 1777.

Catherine McCall and her father returned to Virginia in 1783, where she later made use of her inherited wealth and her father's business experience to embark on a long business career of her own. At the end of the eighteenth century, she enslaved the largest number of people of any white person in Essex County, and by the time she died in 1828, she had founded and run two ironmaking firms, one in Richmond and one in Alexandria, both of which used the labor of enslaved men and women whom she owned. Catherine McCall never married. Very few Virginians recovered and prospered to that extent after their families were divided because of the War for Independence.

23

Live As If Free

In June 1782, the General Assembly received a petition from thirty-three residents of Henrico County, which included the town of Richmond, the new capital of the state. The petition is preserved in the Records of the General Assembly, Legislative Petitions, Henrico County, Record Group 78, Library of Virginia.

The petitioners complained in a long and complex run-on sentence "that many Persons have suffer'd"—permitted—"their Slaves to go about to hire themselves and pay their Masters for their hire and others under pretence of puting them free set them out to live for themselves and allow their Masters such hire as they can agree on by which means the said Slaves live in a very Idle and disorderly Manner and in order to pay their Master their due hire are frequently Stealing in the Neighbourhood in which they reside or which tends to a worse Consequence encourage the Neighbouring Slaves to steal from their Masters and others, and they become the receivers and Traders of those Goods, haveing time to go at large, and allso gives great discontent to other Slaves who are not alow,d such Indulgencies; it being generally beleiv,d that those Slaves do not labour sufficient to pay their Masters their hire and clothe themselves in an Honest Manner—"

The practice of some enslavers to permit some of their enslaved people to live as if free was not new, and it was not strictly legal, but the petitioners did not succeed in persuading the General Assembly to enact sufficiently strong new laws to halt the practice or to punish enslavers who illegally allowed people to earn their own livings, even if for the purpose of purchasing their freedom. White people submitted complaints such as this one to legislatures, county governments, and city councils through to the end of slavery in the spring of 1865.

Some of the reasons why people believed that the practice should be effectively prohibited appear in the petition from the Henrico County residents: that it could encourage enslaved people to become lazy and refuse to work, even to support themselves independent of slavery; that it could increase the amount of perceived crime that improperly controlled enslaved people could commit; that it would promote a traffic in stolen goods, which would undoubtedly lead to additional thievery; that it would set a dangerous example to enslaved people that it was possible to live as if free.

The apprehensions that animated the petitioners closely resemble fears that upper-class people had always harbored about working-class people generally. Employers of wage laborers, masters of indentured servants or apprentices, and enslavers had selfish reasons to oppose granting leeway to any people who worked for them to live without sufficiently strict supervision or control. Masters and enslavers also believed, perhaps with a certain amount of justification, that the ill consequences of enslaved people living as if free jeopardized both public safety and the system of slavery, itself. But as with the other laws that the General Assembly enacted to prohibit enslaved people from moving about the countryside without passes from their enslavers, or the laws that the assembly enacted early in the nineteenth century to require free Black men and women to register with the local government or risk possible re-enslavement, state and local officials did not uniformly enforce the laws.

One of the reasons must certainly be that some appreciable proportion of the white population did not share all of the apprehensions that motivated the Henrico County petitioners. At times when white people believed that enslaved people or free Black people were restless or plotting to revolt or retaliate against white people, waves of unease or even panic temporarily gripped some communities in Virginia. However, those were usually fairly short-lived episodes, even the most serious ones that produced violence. In those circumstances, white men who held responsible offices in local government or who had the management of large numbers of workers took measures to protect themselves, their families, and their communities, sometimes very rigorous or even violent measures, including strict enforcement of laws that they might have previously ignored.

At other times, some of those same white men and women may have been much less uneasy. People who lived in relatively close proximity knew one another, and it is likely that in a considerable number of instances, white people did not believe that the enslaved or free Black people in their midst were always dangerous. Under that circumstance, it should not be surprising that some white enslavers were willing to allow some of their enslaved people an opportunity to live their own lives, at least part of the time, or to earn money with which to purchase their freedom. In such a case, enslavers did not have to become abolitionists or even opponents of slavery to permit enslaved men and women whom they believed to be honest and industrious to live and labor for themselves so long as the practice did not produce serious financial loss to the enslaver.

During and after the American Revolution, which dramatically spread ideas of liberty and equality—the Revolutionary language of liberty—throughout all classes of society, the number of enslavers who had sympathy for some of the people they enslaved apparently increased, and therefore, the number of enslaved people who were able to live as if free also increased. As the practice became increasingly conspicuous, it could appear to be in the process of becoming more alarming or more dangerous. Whether this particular petition disclosed that the petitioners also had racist views seems somewhat unclear; but they may have believed that Black people were likely to have inferior morals, be more often dishonest than white people, or be less afraid of engaging in illegal or socially disruptive behavior. The close links between slavery as a system of labor and social control and racist ideas about the inferiority of Black people had grown together side by side during the seventeenth and eighteenth centuries. They could have converged here, in this petition, in the apprehensions that the petitioners made known to the General Assembly.

Ideas cut both ways, though. In the same year of 1782 when the petitioners sent their plea to the General Assembly, the legislature enacted a new law that permitted enslavers to emancipate their enslaved people, either individually or as groups. The new law strongly suggests that ideas about liberty and freedom in the Revolutionary language of liberty operated on political leaders as well as on enslaved people and at least some enslavers.

For two decades after passage of the 1782 law, Virginians composed wills or executed and registered deeds of manumission and freed a large number of enslaved people. No source or combination of sources exists to allow for making an accurate estimate, but it appears clear from census data that the federal government began to compile in 1790 that the number of free Black Virginians increased during that time more than would be expected from a natural increase as a result of more births than deaths.

Some famous and influential Virginians freed their enslaved people. George Washington had relied on enslaved laborers all of his adult life as well as on enslaved body servants and household servants. But during the War for Independence and later as the first president of the United States and the most famous of the founding fathers, he came to see that slavery was incompatible with the liberty that the new representative democracy had brought about. Washington therefore provided in his will that all of the enslaved people that he owned outright receive their freedom at the time of the death of his wife. He also instructed the executors of his estate to assist the freed people into freedom. Washington hoped that his actions would serve as a wholesome example to other enslavers to free men, women, and children from bondage. Too few did.

Some had already done so. In Richard Randolph's long will, which he wrote and signed in February 1796, he explained why he provided that some of the many enslaved people he had inherited should be freed and provided with a tract of his land on which they could live and provide for themselves. "In the first place," Randolph began, to make restitution "as far as I am able, to an unfortunate race of bondmen, over whom my ancestors have usurped and exercised the most lawless and monstrous tyranny, and in whom my countrymen (by their iniquitous Laws, in contradiction of their own declaration of rights, and in violation of every sacred Law of nature; of the inherent, unalienable & imprescriptible rights of man; and of every principle of moral & political honesty;) have vested me with absolute power.

"To express my abhorance of the Theory, as well as infamous practices of usurping the rights of our fellow creatures, equally intituled with ourselves to the enjoyment of Liberty and happiness:

"To exculplate myself, to those who may perchance to think or hear of me after death from the black crime, which might otherwise be imputed to me, of voluntarily holding the above mentioned miserable beings in the same state of abject slavery in which I found them on receiving my patrimony, at Lawful age"—that is, enslaved people whom he inherited when he turned twenty-one years old—"To impress my children with just horror at a crime so enormous & indelible, to enjure them in the last words of a fond father never to participate in it, in any the remotest degree, however sanctioned by Laws (framed by the tyrants themselves who oppress them,) or supported by false reason, used always and to soil the sordid views of avarice, and the lust of power."

The largest of the late-eighteenth-century emancipations was that of Robert Carter, a former member of the royal Council of State, who converted from the Church of England to the Baptist Church and then fell under the influence of the idealistic Swedish mystic Emanuel Swedenborg and joined the Church of the New Jerusalem. His new religious beliefs persuaded Carter that slavery was morally intolerable, so when he drafted his will in 1791, he provided for the emancipation of more than 500 men, women, and children.

24

Emigrating to Kentucky

Beginning with Daniel Boone's first exploratory visit to the far western region of Virginia called Kentucky in 1769, Virginians and other Americans moved there in search of new land and new opportunities. Even during the War for Independence, people moved to Kentucky. Between Boone's first explorations and the admission of Kentucky as a new state in 1792, about 60,000 to 65,000 white people moved to Kentucky and took with them between 10,000 and 15,000 enslaved Black people. The population growth was so fast that almost no adult white men who lived in the new state as of 1792 had been born there.

Many young members of old and established Virginia families that had too many sons or too few acres of land found the lure of untilled land in Kentucky too strong to resist. Others whose families had arrived in Virginia more recently also moved to the west. Even though many of the white settlements west of the Blue Ridge Mountains were no more than three or four decades old at the time of independence, some men and women there sought their futures farther west in Kentucky, too.

Annie Henry Christian, of Montgomery County, a sister of Patrick Henry, wrote to Elizabeth Christian Fleming on September 9, 1783. Annie Christian told her sister-in-law that her husband, William Christian, the addressee's brother and a burgess before the war and a colonel during it, had surprised her by returning sooner than she anticipated from his reconnoitering expedition to Kentucky. The letter from Christian to Fleming is in the William Fleming Papers in the library of Washington and Lee University.

"We are all well here thank the Lord," Annie Christian began, "& your dear little Bettsey going to School with all her Cousins very happy." Schools were so rare, perhaps nonexistent, in that part of Virginia that families who could afford it sometimes hired private tutors. In this case, it appears that the Christian and Fleming families, perhaps together with some other relatives or neighbors, pooled their resources to provide a teacher for their children.

Annie Christian continued, "We were surpriz'd last thursday to see Mr. Christian return home so soon, from Kentucky." It was common from the colonial period well into the twentieth century for women when writing or speaking about their husbands to refer to them as Mr., and men often referred to their wives as Mrs., rather than by their first names, even within their immediate families. She also wrote that she was "much shockd when I saw Tom Hody," who might have been an enslaved body servant, "come riding up foremost & alone with his Masters pistols I imeadiately concluded that the Indians had killd Some & chased the rest home, but as soon as Tom spoke smilingly I knew all was well." Christian concluded, "your Brother seems to think Kentucky a rich body of Land, & one acre of Corn there is worth two here & everry Thing else raising in Proportion."

Some members of the Christian, Fleming, and other families from the Valley of Virginia had already moved to Kentucky by then. Elizabeth Fleming's husband had acquired land in Kentucky, too, in spite of the constant danger from First Nations tribes who used the region as hunting grounds.

The passage of white Americans into the west led to many conflicts between settlers and tribes in the area. The Cherokee and other southern tribes had never agreed that Virginians could settle the land south of the Ohio River, and they resisted the migration and sometimes attacked the western settlements or parties of people on the way to settle in the west. In the region of western North Carolina that became northeastern Tennessee, one resident resisted so effectively early in the 1790s that government officials in Richmond singled him out for death. His name appears in government documents as Captain Benge, Bench, Benje, and Benjie. In April 1794, a Virginia militia lieutenant killed and scalped him. The lieutenant's commanding officer sent the scalp to Richmond as proof that Benge was dead and recommended that the General Assembly reward the lieutenant with a fancy new rifle.

Scalping of members of First Nations tribes was probably not common, but from time to time during the seventeenth and eighteenth centuries frontier men sent human scalps to Jamestown, Williamsburg, or Richmond in the same way that men presented crow skins or wolf ears to county courts to collect bounties for destroying what they regarded as harmful animals. Captain Benge's life became legendary in southwestern Virginia, and reports persisted as late as the 1920s that his scalp was still on display in the state Capitol in Richmond. It cannot now be found.

No wonder that Kentucky gained the nickname "the dark and bloody ground."

The dangers did not dissuade the Christian and Fleming families. Annie Henry Christian informed her sister-in-law that one of Fleming's relatives there "was to be married the day after Mr. Christian left her house to Bob Daniel your Brother tried wth every way in his power to break of the Match but to no purpose, he drove the chap of intirely as he Thought, but your Sister found means of corresponding with him & made up matters again. I never say I was even shock'd to hear of her marrying that fellow, he & his Brother were here as they went out & stayd a day or two, & I cou'd not have thought your Sister so capable of being imposed upon by any person whatever—as for Beauty, Scence, Fortune, Family, or Education, he is possessed of niether, as to his temper, I cant say any thing at all."

Separation by emigration to the west cut off regular communication among members of families much as emigration from ancestral homes in Great Britain or Europe (or involuntary immigration from Africa aboard a ship of the infamous international slave trade) had cut off regular communication. In many such cases, family members never saw one another again. Events such as the unexpected marriage that Christian mentioned occurred without what some members undoubtedly believed was sufficient thought or consultation with wiser, elder relatives.

"I think our Selves happy," Annie Christian informed her sister-in-law, returning to other family matters, "to have such a tutor to our children, & hope before long your Bettsey will be able to write you a letter. my dear Girls have told me so much of their good Uncles & your kindness to them in particular, to poor Sally in her Sickness that I think myself under the greatest obligation to both for the tender care you shewd by my poor sick child."

The contents of Annie Christian's letters leave no doubt about the importance of affectionate relationships among members of her extended family, including the relatives of her in-laws. The breaking of those relationships as a result of emigration to Kentucky or anywhere else on the frontier must have produced sadness and worry in her family circle and in those of women and men like her and her sister-in-law. Nevertheless, in spite of the many familiar difficulties of remaining in touch with close relatives and the dangers of the frontier, she and her husband planned to move to the west.

In 1785, Annie and William Christian and their six children moved to Kentucky to try to take advantage of the opportunities that they believed existed in the west. They settled on Beargrass Creek, near the site of the later city of Louisville. The Christians also transported the enslaved people they owned to Kentucky to work the land and to extract salt from a place called Bullet's Lick, or Saltsburg, near the present-day city of Shepherdsville. Because Colonel Christian was one of the more experienced military men in the region, it fell to him to command a militia expedition the next year. He and the men under his command crossed the Ohio River and engaged a party of Wabash warriors. In the fighting that ensued, Christian was killed on April 9, 1786, scarcely a year after he and his family moved from the relative safety of Virginia to the more dangerous frontier in Kentucky.

Annie Christian apparently planned to remain in Kentucky after her husband's death. She wrote to her mother in the spring of 1787: "We are all well thank the Lord, & my little Family as happy as can be expected in our Situation, & thank the Lord we enjoy many blessings in this Strange Country, & have been Supported in an uncomon manner here under our great loss; without friends & a helpless Family, left to the mercy of many Creditors, what cou'd I expect, but ruin & distress, but blessed be God we are likely to Struggle through our difficulties beyond what was looked for, & I hope never to forget the mercies I have experienced in the day of my distress. Oh may I ever be thankfull for supporting Grace—one year & one month is now passd away, since I was deprived of my chief earthly Happiness. I have had a Strange scene since I got to this Country indeed." She and her children relied on the labor of their enslaved men and women to produce food and a cash crop to sustain them.

In September 1788, though, two and a half years after William Christian was killed, Annie Christian with her family and a few of her enslaved people returned to Virginia. We will never know whether the sorrowful sojourn in Kentucky was in part responsible, but by the following year she had developed tuberculosis, what at the time was called consumption. It was a common illness that often resulted in death until the development of antibiotics in the first half of the twentieth century. Perhaps sensing that her end may be approaching, Christian engaged her brother, attorney Patrick Henry, to draft a will for her, and she then sailed, apparently without her children, to Antigua, in the West Indies. She spent the winter there but did not regain her health. The unfortunate woman died on May 4, 1790, shortly after the ship on which she returned to Virginia landed in Norfolk.

25

A Daring Attempt on a Very Important Part of Our Property

IN 1784 AND 1785, 1,244 men in eight counties in central and south-central Virginia signed and submitted petitions to the General Assembly to object to proposals that some Methodists and Baptists had made to emancipate enslaved people in the state. The petitions were part of an organized campaign—the earliest known such campaign in the new state—against the abolition of slavery. We know this because copies of two of the five texts were circulated and signed in more than one county. Men from the counties of Pittsylvania, Mecklenburg, Lunenburg, Hanover, Halifax, Henrico, Brunswick, and Amelia signed the petitions.

The documents are important not only because they are evidence of an organized effort but also because they advanced new arguments in favor of slavery as it had evolved in Virginia during the previous one and two-thirds centuries. The petitions are in the Records of the General Assembly, Legislative Petitions, Record Group 78, Library of Virginia, filed under the names of their counties of origin, and are printed in Fredrika Teute Schmidt and Barbara Ripel Wilhelm, eds., "Early Proslavery Petitions in Virginia," *William and Mary Quarterly,* 3d ser., 30 (1973): 133–46.

The petitioning campaign to defend slavery began in Hanover and Henrico Counties, near Richmond, with three nearly identical petitions that contained a total of 257 signatures. The House of Delegates received them on November 16, 1784. Three copies of a longer petition that 299 men signed in the counties of Pittsylvania, Mecklenburg, and Amelia reached the House of Delegates on November 8 and 10, 1785. Also on November 10, the House received a petition that 266 men signed in Brunswick County and another petition that 261 men in Halifax County signed. In Lunenburg County,

161 men signed an even longer petition that the House received on November 19, 1785, the last of that group of pro-slavery petitions.

The texts of the petitions indicate that the petitioners worried primarily about the influence of the Methodists and Baptists who opposed slavery—not all Methodists and Baptists, by any means, but enough to be worrisome to some enslavers. The petitioners may also have worried about something that Thomas Jefferson proposed not long before. He believed, as a consequence of his unhappy two years as governor during the war, when his responsibilities far exceeded his constitutional capacity to act, that the Virginia Constitution of 1776 should be revised and replaced. He had lamented the undemocratic nature of the constitution from the beginning and prepared a draft for a new constitution. How widely knowledge of his proposal got spread about is not clear, but one provision in it could have fueled the anxieties of the 1,244 men who signed the proslavery petitions in 1784 and 1785. Jefferson proposed that all people born on or after January 1, 1800, be born free, which would gradually eliminate slavery in Virginia as the generations of enslaved people then living died out. Under the plan that Jefferson proposed, which resembled plans that some northern states later adopted, slavery in Virginia could have lasted until the latter years of the nineteenth century but would almost certainly have been extinguished by the twentieth.

The petition that 261 men signed in Halifax County is more or less representative. It began, "When the British Parliament usurped a Right to dispose of our Property without our Consent"—when Parliament levied direct taxes on American colonists who were not represented in Parliament—"we dissolved the Union with our Parent Country, & established a Constitution and Form of Government of our own, that our Property might be secure in Future. In Order to effect this, we risked our Lives & fortunes, and waded through Seas of Blood, Divine Providence smiled on our Enterprize, and crowned it with Success. And our Rights of Liberty and Property are now as well secured to us, as they can be by an human Constitution & Form of Government."

Notwithstanding the sacrifices they and other Virginians had made to secure their rights and liberties, the petitioners complained, "a very subtle and daring Attempt is on Foot to deprive us of a very important Part of our Property. An Attempt carried on by the Enemies of our Country, Tools of the British Administration, and supported by a Number of deluded Men among us, to wrest from us our Slaves by an Act of the Legislature for a general Emancipation of them. They have the Address"—boldness—"indeed to cover their Design, with the Veil of Piety and Liberality of Sentiment. But it is unsupported by the Word of God, and will be ruinous to Individuals and to the Public."

The Halifax County petitioners and the men who signed the other petitions defended slavery as an institution that had firm biblical sanction. Eradication of slavery, the Halifax County men argued, "is unsupported by the Word of God. Under the Old Testament Dispensation, Slavery was permitted by the Deity himself." The petitioners quoted Leviticus, chapter 25, verses 44–46: "Both thy Bond-men, and Bond-maids, which thou shalt have, shall be of the Heathen that are round about you; of them shall ye buy Bond-men and Bond-maids. Moreover, of the Children of the Strangers, that do sojourn among you of them shall ye buy, and of their Families that are with you, which they beget in your Land, and they shall be your Possession, and ye shall take them, as an Inheritance for your Children after you, to inherit them for a Possession; they shall be your Bond-men forever."

The petitioners reasoned from that premise, "This Permission to possess and inherit Bond Servants, we have Reason to conclude, was continued through all the Revolutions of the Jewish Government, down to the Advent of our Lord. And we do not find, that either he or his Apostles abridged it. On the Contrary, the Freedom which the Followers of Jesus were taught to expect, was a Freedom from the Bondage of Sin and Satan, and from the Dominion of their Lusts and Passions; but as to their outward Condition, whatever that was, whether Bond or Free, when they embraced Christianity, it was to remain the same afterwards." The petitioners then cited Paul in 1 Corinthians, chapter 7, verses 20 and 24: "Let every Man abide in the same Calling, wherein he is called" and "Let every Man wherein he is called therein abide with God." Thus, the petitioners concluded, the attempt to abolish slavery "is unsupported by the Divine Word."

The petitioners were not the first people to attempt to square the Bible or the institutions and practices of ancient slavery with slavery as it had evolved in Virginia and elsewhere in North America, but they may have broken new ground in suggesting that the Bible effectively discouraged or even prohibited opposition to slavery. They repeated secular reasons in opposition to the abolition of slavery, too. "It is also ruinous to Individuals & to the Public," the Halifax County petitioners continued, "For it involves in it, and is productive of Want, Poverty, Distress, and Ruin to the Free Citizen; Neglect, Famine, and Death to the helpless black Infant & superannuated Parent; the Horrors of all the Rapes, Murders, and Outrages, which a vast Multitude of unprincipled, unpropertied, vindictive, and remorseless Banditti are capable of perpetrating;—inevitable Bankruptcy to the Revenue, and consequently Breach of public Faith, and Loss of Credit with foreign nations;—and lastly Ruin to this now free and flourishing Country."

The petitioners bluntly demanded that the General Assembly "discountenance and utterly reject every Motion and Proposal for emancipating our Slaves; that as the Act lately made" in 1782 "empowering the Owners of Slaves to liberate them, has been and is still productive, in some Measure, of sundry of the above pernicious Effects, you will immediately and totally repeal it, and that as many of the Slaves, liberated by the said Act, have been guilty of Thefts and Outrages, Insolences and Violences destructive to the Peace, Safety, and Happiness of Society, you will make effectual Provision for the due Government of them."

The General Assembly did not do any of the things that the petitioners insisted on, even though slavery was then of the utmost importance to the economy of the state and to the very households of almost every influential public man. For about two decades, the Revolutionary language of liberty and the self-interest of enslavers divided the body politic. In the end, though, as the generation of men and women who lived through the American Revolution and personally remembered the power of that language died out, so too died out the antislavery implications of that language. Early in the nineteenth century, the General Assembly made it more difficult for people to emancipate their enslaved people and for people thus freed to remain in Virginia.

The racism that is evident in the language of the Halifax County petitioners about the dangerous behavior of "a vast Multitude of unprincipled, unpropertied, vindictive, and remorseless Banditti" triumphed over the idealism of the Revolutionary language of liberty. By the middle of the nineteenth century the victory of racism over the ideals of universal individual liberty was virtually complete. When elected Virginians met in convention early in 1861 to debate what the state should do during the secession crisis, not one of more than 150 men spoke a single syllable critical of slavery.

Instead, a large majority of delegates clearly wanted to preserve Virginia as a slave state within the old Union; but as the moment of crisis approached in the spring of that year and civil war began, they decided that slavery would be safer in Virginia if Virginia became one of the Confederate States rather than if it remained one of the United States.

26

Thomas Jefferson, Racist

About the time that the men from Halifax and the other counties submitted their pro-slavery petitions to the General Assembly in 1785, Thomas Jefferson published his book *Notes on the State of Virginia*. He had begun the project in 1780 when he received a series of questions that a French diplomat in Philadelphia submitted to him. While Jefferson was serving as an American diplomat in Paris in 1785, he authorized publication of a limited edition of the book. A French translation appeared two years later, and several printers published English-language editions of *Notes on the State of Virginia* during the ensuing years.

Members of Jefferson's family provided his first biographer with a story that Jefferson had told them. Jefferson recalled that his earliest memory was of being handed up when he was quite young to the care of an enslaved person who carried him on a pillow on horseback as the family traveled from one place to another. The memory is evocative and also symbolic. Throughout Jefferson's entire life, enslaved people and their labor carried him, as if on an easy cushion, through an excellent education, to wealth, to political and diplomatic achievements of the highest order, and to lasting fame as one of the founders of the American republic. His ideas about slavery and about enslaved people evolved to become in direct conflict with his words in the Declaration of Independence that "all men are created equal" and entitled to "life, liberty, and the pursuit of happiness."

Historians and other people sometimes come in for serious criticism when they characterize Jefferson as a racist and therefore indirectly as an apologist for slavery or racial discrimination. Rather than rely on what other people wrote about Jefferson, it is best, in order to understand Jefferson's ideas, to read what he, himself, wrote and published in *Notes on the State of Virginia*.

Jefferson wrote some of the most eloquent and memorable language in defense of human liberty of any American of any time. In *Notes on the State of Virginia* he also wrote some of the first and most objectionable language that laid out the basis for the scientific racism of the nineteenth and twentieth centuries that openly branded people of African birth or ancestry as inferior to people of European birth or ancestry or even as subhuman animals of a separate creation. The opinions on that subject that Jefferson included in *Notes on the State of Virginia* provided a basis for defending American slavery on racist grounds and later for the Jim Crow regime of racial segregation and discrimination in the twentieth-century United States.

In *Notes on the State of Virginia,* Jefferson recognized the injustice of slavery and wrote, "I tremble for my country, when I reflect that God is just: that his justice cannot sleep for ever." If the grievances of enslaved people ever led them to rise up and revolt against the enslavers, he acknowledged, "God has no attribute which can take side with us in such a contest."

Jefferson also recognized that slavery was harmful to people, but what he wrote about was how it was harmful to white people, to enslavers, and not to enslaved people. "The whole commerce between master and slave," he wrote in another passage in the book, "is a perpetual exercise of the most boisterous passions, the most unremitting despotism on the one part, and degrading submissions on the other." He continued, "Our children see this and learn to imitate it; for man is an imitative animal. This quality is the germ of all education in him. From his cradle to his grave he is learning to do what he sees others do. If a parent could find no motive either in his philanthropy or in his self-love, for restraining the intemperance of passion towards his slave, it should always be a sufficient one that his child is present. But generally it is not sufficient. The parent storms, the child looks on, catches the lineaments of wrath, puts on the same airs in the circle of smaller slaves, gives a loose to his worst of passions, and thus nursed, educated, and daily exercised in tyranny, cannot but be stamped by it with odious peculiarities. The man must be a prodigy who can retain his manners and morals undepraved by such circumstances."

Whether Jefferson's commentary was purely theoretical or partly autobiographical is not possible to state. Evidence does not exist from his childhood to demonstrate clearly whether the causes and consequences of the domestic tyranny of the enslaver over enslaved people that he described derived from his personal experiences or observations or merely from his general deductions about the commonplace behaviors of white owners of Black people. Jefferson was undoubtedly a witness to and a participant in some of the physical violence that maintaining slavery required, as well as to the permanent separation of members of enslaved families from one another through sales or the leasing of laborers to distant places where other men needed additional workers. Jefferson's comments included virtually nothing about what Black people may have thought and learned from the effects of white people's treatment of them. What Jefferson wrote exhibited virtually no sympathy for, or understanding of, the plight of enslaved people.

After Jefferson included a gradual emancipation provision in his draft for a new state constitution early in the 1780s, he made no other proposals to abolish slavery by any method. Jefferson toyed from time to time with schemes to alleviate some of the worst aspects of slavery. He also proposed colonizing freed Black people to other parts of the world, if anybody could devise a means of ending slavery, but he always concluded that society could not afford the expense. Jefferson also believed that fairness to enslavers required that they be compensated for the value of their property if slavery were abolished, either gradually or speedily; but neither he nor anybody else was willing to pay for that compensation or personally suffer the financial losses to be incurred by an uncompensated termination of slavery.

"It will probably be asked," Jefferson replied in *Notes on the State of Virginia* to anticipated questions about the peaceful cohabitation of free white and free Black Americans if colonization were not a viable option, "Why not retain and incorporate the blacks into the state, and thus save the expence of supplying, by importation of white settlers, the vacancies they will leave?" The answer to that question, he explained, was that "Deep rooted prejudices entertained by the whites; ten thousand recollections, by the blacks, of the injuries they have sustained; new provocations; the real distinctions which nature has made; and many other circumstances, will divide us into parties, and produce convulsions which will probably never end but in the extermination of the one or the other race." A grim deduction if ever there were one.

A key to understanding why Jefferson understood the predicament as he did is in the phrase "the real distinctions which nature has made." He continued his explanation and opened for future generations the main line of reasoning of the scientific racists based on "the real distinctions" that everybody could see. "The first difference which strikes us is that of colour," Jefferson wrote. That color was "fixed in nature, and it is as real as if its seat and cause were better known to us." Color was an observable difference, and Jefferson used that visible natural phenomenon to help explain other differences, as if they, too, were naturally occurring differences, and all to the disadvantage of people of African birth or with African ancestry.

"And is this difference of no importance?" he asked rhetorically. Of course it was, he answered himself. Jefferson then advanced his argument and explanation with several other examples that reflected his belief in the natural or cultural superiority of white people over Black people. He began, "Is it not the foundation of a greater or less share of beauty in the two races? Are not the fine mixtures of red and white, the expressions of every passion by greater or less suffusions of colour in the one, preferable to that eternal monotony, which reigns in the countenances, that immoveable veil of black which covers all the emotions of the other race?" Jefferson rooted his standard of beauty firmly and exclusively in contemporary western European tastes and values.

"Add to these," Jefferson continued, "flowing hair, a more elegant symmetry of form, their own judgment in favour of the whites, declared by the preference of them, as uniformly as is the preference of the Oron-ootan"—orangutans and the other great apes—"for the black women over those of his own species." Jefferson there repeated what he had read in some rather fanciful natural histories, that in some parts of Africa and Asia, inferior ape-like creatures lusted sexually after the more attractive females of superior creatures, white people. And that in turn indicates that he may have believed something that later racists often repeated, that inferior Black men had a dangerous natural lust for superior white women.

Without breaking his line of argument so much as even to begin a new paragraph, Jefferson continued in the same vein: "The circumstance of superior beauty, is thought worthy of attention in the propagation of our horses, dogs, and other domestic animals; why not in that of man?" He then slipped the word *other* in the next sentence to link horses, dogs, farm animals, and people, Black enslaved laborers. "Besides those of colour, figure, and hair, there are other physical distinctions proving a difference of race. They have less hair on the face and body" than white people, as if that were a mark of a less favored population than Europeans and their descendants. "They secrete less by the kidnies, and more by the glands of the skin, which gives them a very strong and disagreeable odour. This greater degree of transpiration renders them more tolerant of heat, and less so of cold, than the whites."

Alongside and in addition to obvious physical differences between Black people and white people, Jefferson enumerated behavioral and intellectual differences, all of which he described as innate and all also to the disadvantage of inferior Africans and their descendants. "They seem to require less sleep" than white people. "A black, after hard labour through the day, will be induced by the slightest amusements to sit up till midnight, or later, though knowing he must be out with the first dawn of the morning. They are at least as brave, and more adventuresome. But this may perhaps proceed from a want of fore-thought, which prevents their seeing a danger till it be present. When present, they do not go through it with more coolness or steadiness than the whites."

Again, "They are more ardent after their female: but love seems with them to be more an eager desire"—an animal lust—"than a tender delicate mixture of sentiment and sensation." European men, for Jefferson, were the standard by which he judged in that explanation, which completely ignored the emotions and feelings of all women, whether European, African, or First Nations.

"Their griefs," Jefferson continued, "are transient. Those numberless afflictions, which render it doubtful whether heaven has given life to us in mercy or in wrath, are less felt, and sooner forgotten with them. In general, their existence appears to participate more of sensation than reflection. To this must be ascribed their disposition to sleep when abstracted from their diversions, and unemployed in labour." Jefferson directly contradicted what he had just written in the same paragraph about the desire and ability of enslaved people to stay awake and even to sing and dance late into the night after a hard day of working in the fields. The contradiction, which he clearly failed to detect, disclosed that he probably believed that Black people were inherently indolent and therefore less socially valuable and probably less individually responsible than white people.

But that was not all. Comparing Black people and white people "by their faculties of memory, reason, and imagination," Jefferson continued, "it appears to me, that in memory they are equal to the whites; in reason much inferior, as I think one could scarcely be found capable of tracing and comprehending the investigations of Euclid; and that in imagination they are dull, tasteless, and anomalous." He then admitted the possibility that free people in Africa might exhibit different or superior behaviors and talents than enslaved people in America exhibited, and that it was not possible to discover if the hard work and living conditions of slavery debased their natural talents or whether their inability to learn more from their superiors indicated the outermost boundaries of their natural abilities.

Jefferson inclined toward the latter explanation and wrote that Black people "might have availed themselves of the conversation of their masters; many have been brought up to the handicraft arts, and from that circumstance have always been associated with the whites. Some have been liberally educated, and all have lived in countries where the arts and sciences are cultivated to a considerable degree, and have had before their eyes samples of the best works from abroad."

Then, Jefferson made a sharp distinction that indicated that he believed that on the whole Black people had failed to learn from—could not learn from?—their betters. "The Indians," he wrote, "with no advantages of this kind, will often carve figures on their pipes not destitute of design and merit. They will crayon out an animal, a plant, or a country, so as to prove the existence of a germ in their minds which only wants cultivation. They astonish you with strokes of the most sublime oratory; such as prove their reason and sentiment strong, their imagination glowing and elevated. But never yet could I find that a black had uttered a thought above the level of plain narration; never seen even an elementary trait of painting or sculpture."

In music, Jefferson admitted, Black people appeared to be "more generally gifted than the whites with accurate ears for tune and time," but that was the sole distinction he enumerated in favor of Black people, and one that closely resembled later characterizations of Black people as being particularly musical, perhaps because they were not intellectual or genuinely artistic by western European standards; and music might have been regarded then as a more primitive art.

Jefferson concluded his enumeration of the innate incapacities of Black people by writing, "Misery is often the parent of the most affecting touches in poetry:—Among the blacks is misery enough, God knows, but no poetry.

Love is the peculiar œstrum of the poet. Their love is ardent, but it kindles the senses only, not the imagination." Jefferson implied that among Africans and their descendants, the sex drive, not love, motivated them, as sex, not love, motivated the mating behavior of all other animals that were inferior to white human beings.

Jefferson wrote all that in the 1780s, a few years after he composed the Declaration of Independence with its Revolutionary language of liberty and before he concluded his long residence in France and witnessed the outbreak of the French Revolution. He wrote all that before he apparently began a long sexual relationship with one of the people he enslaved, Sally Hemings, a young half-sister of Jefferson's late wife. Very strong circumstantial evidence indicates that they had several children. No plausible circumstantial evidence and no physical evidence at all indicates that any other white, male member of Thomas Jefferson's immediate family was present at the times when Hemings is known to have become pregnant. Which raises, but does not provide answers for, other questions: Did that long physical relationship become a loving, emotional relationship? Did that relationship, whatever it was, modify the harsh beliefs with which Jefferson characterized people of African birth or descent when he wrote *Notes on the State of Virginia* in the 1780s?

From all of Jefferson's documented comments and actions, the answer, sadly, appears to be no. He did not soften his ideas about the inferiority of Africans and their descendants, nor with one exception did he ever take any consequential steps toward ameliorating the condition of any of the enslaved people whom he owned. The exception is also an argument in favor of his paternity of Sally Hemings's children. Jefferson allowed a few of those children to enjoy favored status at Monticello or to escape from slavery and, because of their being one-sixteenth or less of African ancestry, to pass invisibly into white society elsewhere.

In a private letter that Jefferson wrote in 1815, he calculated with algebraic formulae that "a 4th cross of one race of animals with another gives an issue equivalent for all sensible purposes to the original blood." And according to Virginia law, "2 crosses with the pure white, and a 3^{d} with any degree of mixture, however small," was sufficient for "clearing the issue of the negro blood." By that calculation, Sally Hemings's children, if they were also Thomas Jefferson's children, were legally and perhaps otherwise no longer Black, but Virginia law decreed that they remained legally enslaved.

It is of no small importance to notice, too, the choice of the verb *clearing* in Jefferson's description of the manner in which repeated matings of descendants of African natives with superior white people cleared the blot or stigma of the African ancestry and made the fourth and fifth generations virtually equivalent to white people but without changing their legal status if they were enslaved.

Jefferson also never did anything or wrote anything after he published *Notes on the State of Virginia* to promote the end of slavery in Virginia or in the new nation. Indeed, he repeatedly refused even to endorse the proposals of other men with the feeble excuse that such work was the responsibility of younger generations than his, even though his own generation, of which he was a conspicuous leader, had failed at that task when it had the best opportunity to exploit the Revolutionary language of liberty that Jefferson, more than any other person, created and popularized.

Slavery did not have to persist and flourish in the southern states as it did. It could have been very different, and therefore the entire history of North America would have been different. "For of all sad words of tongue or pen," John Greenleaf Whittier wrote in 1856 when slavery flourished in fifteen of the United States of America, "The saddest are these: 'It might have been.'"

27

The Genius of Republican Government

AT THE CENTER OF all of the discussions about independence, the resulting revolution, and the formation of new state and national constitutions during the Revolutionary period was the concept of republican, or representative, government. By the term *republican,* late-eighteenth-century Americans meant what we refer to as a representative democracy, in which elected representatives act on behalf of the whole people.

The words *republican* and *democrat* as Americans used them in the eighteenth century do not have any direct relation to the political parties of later centuries that chose those words to be names of partisan political organizations. So many changes have taken place in the meantime that the meanings and implications of the words have evolved, even though political parties adopted those venerable words to identify their policies. The parties and the policies have themselves also changed.

In a limited sense, the British government was representative in that a small number of prosperous males elected members of the House of Commons, who represented the whole realm. But nobody elected members of the House of Lords, and all of the executive powers of government and the appointment of judges for courts of law lay in the hands of a hereditary king and his ministers.

The constitutional revolution that began in North America with the expulsion of the king from the governments of thirteen British colonies required adult, white men who owned property to fashion new structures of state government and establish a new national government. The Virginia Constitution of 1776 effectively abolished or severely restricted the authority of almost all of the institutions that monarchy had created and enlarged the scope of authority of the elected representatives in the General Assembly. Except for the abolition of the office of king, the new constitution changed surprisingly little in the manner in which government in the new state functioned.

The General Assembly remained the only elective body in Virginia, but the constitution authorized voters to elect members of a new Senate as well as members of the House of Delegates, which succeeded to the role of the old House of Burgesses. The constitution endowed the assembly with authority to elect the governor annually but prevented the election of any one person to more than three consecutive one-year terms or from electing that person governor again until he had been out of office for at least four years. The assembly also elected an advisory Council of State and required that the governor have the approval of the members of the council before he could act. The constitution empowered the assembly to elect all of the judges and prohibited any person other than a county justice of the peace from exercising legislative, executive, and judicial powers simultaneously.

The constitution left in place the undemocratic county courts on which men served lifetime appointments. The constitution prevented the governor from appointing justices of the peace to fill vacancies on the courts except from lists of names that the courts submitted to him; so the county courts remained, as they had always been, unelected, self-perpetuating boards with extensive local executive, legislative, and judicial authority. So, too, the unelected vestries of the parishes of the Church of England, which remained a part of the government of Virginia until the passage of the Act for Establishing Religious Freedom in 1786; and during that time, the government remained part of the church.

Each state configured its new government in its own way. As in Virginia, many of them made minimal changes to the institutions and practices that they had developed during the colonial period. Every state government, as well as the Articles of Confederation that Congress created to be the new national government, was based on the theory of republican government.

Virtually nobody at the time advocated actual democracy, rule by the people. The societies of the colonies had been hierarchical, and for the most part, the societies of the new states were, too. At that time, the words *democracy* and *freedom* suggested anarchy and chaos. Revolutionary Americans usually used the words *republican* and *liberty* to indicate a less egalitarian, well-ordered civilized society.

In keeping with the implications of the Revolutionary language of liberty, the people of each state also faced requests or demands for an extension of the right to vote to a larger number of people or for modification of institutions of government to make them more republican, more representative. An early episode in the long campaigns that Virginians waged to expand the representative character of their governments began with the preparation in Norfolk of two petitions to the General Assembly sometime in the summer or autumn of 1786. The House of Delegates received both petitions on November 10 of that year. They are preserved in the Records of the General Assembly, Legislative Petitions, Norfolk Borough, Record Group 78, Library of Virginia, and printed in Brent Tarter, ed., *The Order Book and Related Papers of the Common Hall of the Borough of Norfolk, Virginia, 1736–1798* (Richmond, 1979), 241–43.

The first petition, which 112 residents of Norfolk signed, complained that their city, which was legally a borough, a name that made no essential difference in its operations, functioned under a charter that Governor William Gooch had issued in the name of King George II in 1736 and that it was not a republican government. Under the charter, as the petitioners explained it, the mayor, aldermen, and members of the common council "Hold their offices during life, That they fill up vacancies as they Happen without the voice of the free holders, Citizens, and free men of the said borough, That they impose Taxes on your petitioners without their consent, Which is contrary to the rights of free citizens And opposite to the genius of a Republican Government.—" Taxation without representation had been one of the primary causes of American resistance to acts of Parliament that led to independence.

The petitioners asked the General Assembly to "annul and make void Alter or amend the present Charter of the Borough of Norfolk; And grant to them a new Charter, Securing to them the same rights and privileges, as your Honourable House have granted, to other incorporated cities & towns within this Commonwealth, since we became a free and independent people." One of the many powers that the General Assembly of Virginia in effect inherited as a result of the exclusion of the king from the government of the new state was authority to issue charters of incorporation to create new municipal governments, to create corporations to raise money and construct canals and toll roads, or to form new educational institutions. The petitioners from Norfolk believed that the General Assembly therefore had power to annul or change the charter that the royal governor had issued in the name of the king half a century earlier, in 1736, and create a new form of municipal government that, like the few new cities that the state had created since the war began, had a republican, or elected, representative government.

The petitioners concluded with a plea that the assembly would "set such bounds to the Charter, as shall for ever secure to the citizens, Good Order, Government, Liberty, and every Privilege and Franchise, that we have a right to claim under the Laws and Protection of our present constitution."

The officials of the municipal government of Norfolk and some other citizens filed a counterpetition that the House of Delegates received on the same day. Those petitioners asked that the legislature make no changes to the form of the city government. Rather than defend the unelected, unrepublican character of the city government, they argued that the public officials of Norfolk had done their jobs well and that therefore the city needed no change. The petitioners stated that "if their proceedings in the police of the corporation from it's commencement, cou'd be laid before the General Assembly that, they wou'd merit the approbation of the Legislature," and that therefore there was no need to make any changes. The word *police* in that sentence meant the laws and the administration of public policies, not law enforcement officers.

Then, still not defending the unelected nature of the city government, the petitioners attacked the characters of the petitioners who asked for change. "Your Memorialists cannot help observing," they complained, "that the petition originates from the opposition of many of its signers, to a law of the Corporation, for the restraint of tippling houses"—bars, or drinking establishments—"that many who have sign'd the petition for making void the Charter, are persons who in violation of the laws of the land, as well as those of the corporation have dared to keep tippling houses to the prejudice of the community at large, and in particular to the Corporation."

Again, "Your Memorialists are informed that the petitioners complain of arbitrary measures taken by the body corporate. Your Memorialists deny that any such arbitrary proceedings have been committed by the body corporate, and request that the petitioners may be called on to declare, in what instance the body corporate have acted illegally." The original petitioners had not, in fact, adduced any acts of arbitrary misgovernment in Norfolk unless all governmental actions that unelected officials took could be so considered; but that did not deter the defenders of the established institutions from charging that changes of the kind that the first petition proposed would lead to deplorable consequences.

"Your Memorialists further observe," they concluded, "that from their situation for business in the community," that is, as a major national seaport, "the people of all Nations have intercourse with them and unless your Memorialists are authorised by an Act of the Legislature to pass bye Laws for their own internal Government, it will always be in the power of disorderly and evil disposed persons, to counteract the intentions of the body corporate, for the preservation of order and good Government. Your Memorialists hope that the privileges of the body corporate will be preserved to them; and farther, that such powers may be granted for the improvement of their police as to the Legislature shall seem meet"—that is, proper.

It is interesting that the petitioners who opposed change did not challenge the claim of the first petitioners that the city government that had been created under royal authority was incompatible with "the genius of a Republican Government." So firmly established by then were the new idea and the ideals of representative government that the defenders of the status quo resorted to character assassination and fearmongering rather than to rational, theoretical, political, or legal arguments to achieve their objective. That tells us much about the power of the Revolutionary language of liberty and the ideals of representative government. Just as many other people in the new nation believed, the defenders of the old charter feared that too much democracy and too much freedom would inevitably lead to chaos and anarchy. They also feared, but did not mention, that a new charter could eliminate or severely restrict the abilities of the sitting aldermen and councilmen to govern the city as they wished and without any restraints from the residents.

At the next session of the General Assembly, in December 1787, the legislature passed An Act to Amend the Charter of the Borough of Norfolk. It authorized qualified voters to elect sixteen members of the common council, each to serve a three-year term. The new charter granted the elected councilmen the "sole and exclusive right of passing bye-laws and taxing the freeholders and inhabitants of the said borough, together with the appropriation of all monies belonging to the same." It authorized the governor to appoint judges of the court of hustings, comparable to the governor's appointment of justices of the peace for county courts, and it permitted the unelected aldermen to retain their offices.

The act of 1787 was a small gain for republican government in one place in Virginia. Unelected aldermen, judges, and county justices of the peace throughout Virginia remained free to continue to govern their localities after that one municipal reform very much as they had before. Advocates for extending the practices of republican government to additional governmental institutions had a long fight. When from time to time the General Assembly chartered a new city, it usually allowed the qualified men there to vote for at least some local officials, but uniformity did not characterize the early municipal charters that the assembly issued then or for a long time thereafter.

The Virginia Constitutional Convention of 1829–30 made almost no changes of consequence other than to permit a small increase in the number of adult, white men who could vote for members of the General Assembly. Not until ratification of the Virginia Constitution of 1851, a full seventy-five years after George Mason and Thomas Jefferson had proclaimed in the Virginia Declaration of Rights and the Declaration of Independence that all men were born equal, did something approaching full equality of voting rights for all white men finally come to Virginia. Black men had to wait until 1867, and all women had to wait until 1920.

28

The Majority, the Minority, and the Constitution

On September 17, 1787, George Washington, as one of his last tasks as president of the Constitutional Convention that met in Philadelphia that year, sent the Constitution that the convention had prepared to the president of Congress in order that it could be submitted to the states for ratification or rejection. Washington characterized the compromises that produced the new Constitution as "the result of that mutual deference and concession, which the peculiarity of our political situation rendered indispensable." Washington explained that the proposed Constitution could not be expected to "meet the full and entire Approbation of every State," but he recommended that "each will doubtless consider that had her Interests been alone consulted the Consequences might have been particularly disagreeable or injurious to others. That it is liable to as few Exceptions as could reasonably have been expected we hope and believe. That it may promote the lasting Welfare of that Country so dear to us all and secure her Freedom and Happiness is our most ardent wish." Washington's letter to the president of Congress is in the Records of the Federal Convention, Record Group 360, National Archives and Records Administration, and is published in W. W. Abbot et al., eds., *Papers of George Washington, Confederation Series,* 6 vols. (Charlottesville, 1992–97): 5:330–31.

The proposed Constitution was a collection of compromises that the majority of the convention delegates hoped would permit the states to remain united in a stronger governmental union than had been the case since ratification of the Articles of Confederation created the first national government during the War for Independence. The compromises required the states to yield on points that some of their leading men and their members of the convention had believed important to them. As Washington indicated, the compromises would not please everybody, but he hoped that their shared objective of securing permanent "Freedom and Happiness" to the nation that he and they had helped found would reconcile enough men to the disappointment that some of them undoubtedly felt.

Opinions about the proposed Constitution varied widely. Some Americans regarded it as creating a too-powerful national government that would endanger the independence of the states or that would overpower the states and lead toward a dangerous consolidation of power in a new national government. Others regarded the proposed new form of government as still inadequate to the task of uniting the country permanently. And the many compromises on matters of detail left sour tastes in many mouths.

In fact, it is something of a wonder that the convention was able to agree at all on the numerous and important compromises. Some compromises adjusted differences between states with large populations and states with small populations, states with claims to large amounts of western land and states with none, and states where slavery was of great importance and states where it was not. One compromise gave each state equal representation in the new United States Senate and representation proportional to its population in the House of Representatives. Other compromises specified how Congress could levy taxes, and how to count inhabitants—the famous three-fifths compromise being the most controversial in that it provided for counting enslaved people at three-fifths of their total number for computing allocation of taxes among the states and for calculating how many representatives each state should have in Congress.

Those issues and others arose during the Virginia Ratification Convention of 1788, which met in Richmond in June when elected delegates from throughout the state discussed the details of the draft Constitution and also the largest of all issues: whether the structure of the new government would safely preserve liberty or lead to an overpowerful national state, and whether the powers that it authorized Congress to exercise and the limitations that it imposed on those powers were adequate to the purpose of strengthening the national government, but not too much. Able as the debaters were, few delegates changed their minds during the convention. As predicted, the final vote was close, 89 to 79 in favor of ratification. The convention then adopted a long list of amendments that it suggested be made to the Constitution as soon as possible in order to secure individual liberties and to preserve the rights of the states, as well as to modify some of the structural features of the Constitution.

The debates in the Virginia Convention were the most thoroughly reported of any ratification convention in the new country and undoubtedly exceeded any other in learned and searching inquiry. A stenographer recorded the speeches and published them. With the exceptions of George Washington, who remained at home at Mount Vernon, and of Thomas Jefferson, who was serving as an American diplomat in France at the time, almost every important public man in Virginia was present

James Madison, who had one of the largest roles in drafting the Constitution in Philadelphia, led the delegates who favored ratification. Governor Edmund Randolph and Henry "Light Horse Harry" Lee, a hero of the War for Independence, argued forcefully for ratification, even though Randolph had refused to sign the Constitution at the end of the Convention of 1787 because several of its provisions displeased him. During the autumn of 1787 and into the winter he advocated calling another convention to try again. When the Virginia Convention began early in June 1788, though, Randolph announced that with no chance of a second convention, he would vote for ratification because the proposed Constitution, even with its faults, was much better than taking no action at all, precisely what George Washington had recommended and hoped for.

Patrick Henry, William Grayson, and George Mason led the opposition. Mason had also refused to sign the Constitution in Philadelphia and published a long list of objections to theoretical and structural aspects of the draft, all of which he believed were fatal. The first of Mason's objections was that the document included no bill of rights. As principal author of the Virginia Declaration of Rights in 1776, it is not surprising that he believed that the new national Constitution should include a corresponding list of liberties that the new government could not endanger, such as freedom of the press, freedom of religion, the right to jury trials, and procedural safeguards for people involved in trials. Mason also objected to many other features of the Constitution.

Ratification of the Constitution of the United States in June 1788 represents, to many people, the conclusion of the American Revolution, which created a new republican form of government for a new nation. Not everyone at the time agreed that ratification was wise, and some of them feared that the new Constitution would destroy the new democratic republic. Disappointed opponents of the Constitution continued for their own various reasons to hope for changes that would amplify, modify, or reduce some of the powers that it gave to the new government. The arguments that Mason and many other men in Virginia and elsewhere made for inclusion of a bill of rights led the First Congress to submit a proposed bill of rights to the states for ratification. At the time of ratification of the Constitution of the United States in 1788, men could not know that Congress would propose a bill of rights, and other men who remained opposed to the Constitution for various reasons continued to agitate for a second national Constitutional Convention.

Patrick Henry anticipated that some of his fellow convention delegates who opposed ratification would refuse to accept the result if the Virginia Convention ratified the Constitution. Shortly before the final vote, he announced that he would accept the result peacefully. "If I shall be in the minority," he informed the other members of the convention, "I shall have those painful sensations, which arise from a conviction of being overpowered in a good cause. Yet I will be a peaceable citizen! I shall therefore patiently wait in expectation of seeing that Government changed so as to be compatible with the safety, liberty and happiness of the people."

Acquiescence in the will of the majority is of the utmost importance in a republic, in a representative democracy of the kind that the Constitutions of Virginia and of the United States had created. Not everybody was willing to accept the result, however, chief among them Henry's powerful ally in the convention, George Mason. Almost immediately after the convention adjourned, Mason called a meeting of opponents of ratification to make plans for future action.

Henry declined to attend for the reasons that he had already stated. Former governor Benjamin Harrison, who had signed the Declaration of Independence and also been a delegate to the Virginia Convention, went to the meeting that Mason called; but when he heard Mason declare that he wanted to organize opposition to the new government that the Constitution created, Harrison walked out. Having lost, he explained, as a Richmond newspaper reported his words, he and his fellow Virginians should "submit as good citizens, until those destructive consequences to their liberty should appear, which the minority apprehended, in which however he hoped they would be mistaken."

The examples of Henry and Harrison helped set a very important precedent that has served the United States that they helped create well when other people followed it but has been very nearly disastrous when they did not.

29

Baptists and the Bill of Rights

RATIFICATION OF THE CONSTITUTION of the United States in June 1788 did not stop debates and disagreements about the document and about the future of representative government in the United States. George Mason was not the only person who found it difficult to reconcile what the men in Norfolk had called "the genius of republican government" with the potentially powerful institutions that the Constitution created. Even men like Patrick Henry and Benjamin Harrison, who acquiesced in the will of the majority of convention delegates, continued to pursue their own ideas and ideals. At the General Assembly session in the winter of 1788–89, which adopted the first law to govern how elections of members of Congress should take place, men who had opposed ratification were in the majority and elected two prominent opponents to the United States Senate: Richard Henry Lee, who had served in the Continental Congress off and on since 1774, and William Grayson, who had spoken powerfully and frequently against ratification in the Virginia Convention.

Other men who had opposed ratification ran for the House of Representatives, including James Monroe, who had served in the Continental Army, in the Continental Congress, and in Europe as a diplomat. As it happened, the man Monroe opposed was James Madison, who had led the advocates of ratification in the convention. They lived in the same new congressional district, which one man charged, without any firm evidence, that Patrick Henry had designed in order that Monroe could defeat Madison and keep the state's foremost supporter of the Constitution out of Congress.

The first popular elections for Congress illustrated how much had changed in Virginia during the years since Virginians united with other colonists to oppose Parliamentary policies. For one thing, people began to ignore the provision in the 1736 election law, which remained in force until the General Assembly revised it in 1785, that made it illegal for a candidate for elective office to advocate or oppose any proposed bill. For another, candidates no longer quietly pretended that they had no political ambitions; they actively sought office. Instead of relying on their local reputations, candidates wrote and spoke to their neighbors in favor of their own political beliefs. In that important respect, the process of electing legislators became more democratic, and the qualified voters had much more influence on public policies than had been the case before the Revolution began. That part of the political revolution occurred with almost no changes to laws but because of changes in people's expectations and behavior.

As a result of those changes, James Madison, for the first time in his public life, had to campaign for election when he was a candidate for the House of Representatives against James Monroe in 1789. The election occurred very early in the year, and during his travels through the large congressional district, Madison got his nose frostbitten. But he won the election and became the legislative leader of the lower House of Congress, where he employed his formidable intellect and the legislative skills that he had honed during the wartime years to unite many of the opponents of ratification with many of its supporters in the creation of the new institutions of government. In the beginning, the first president, George Washington, relied heavily on Madison.

As a member of the House of Representatives, Madison prepared the first draft of what ultimately became the Bill of Rights in 1791. Madison had to change his mind to do so, and the change was almost certainly a direct result of the fact that Madison had to campaign to win election.

Madison had opposed suggestions in the Virginia Convention of 1788 that the absence of a bill of rights from the Constitution was a fatal flaw. According to what he believed and stated in the convention, the draft Constitution did not need a bill of rights because it already contained sufficient protections to prevent Congress or any other part of the federal government from encroaching on any individual or state rights. The separation of powers, the checks and balances, and the compromise that allowed the members of the Senate to represent the states and the members of the House of Representatives to represent the people each separately and

James Madison (1751–1836), by Charles Willson Peale, 1783. (Library of Congress, Prints & Photographs Division)

together guarded against the national government, or any part of it, becoming too strong.

Madison also argued that the Constitution endowed each of the three branches of the government with strictly limited authority, to raise an army and navy, for instance, and to tax certain commercial transactions and people. Nowhere did the Constitution authorize or permit Congress to endanger any fundamental liberty, such as freedom of speech, freedom of the press, or trial by jury. Madison believed that the very structure that he and the other delegates to the Convention of 1787 had created would serve as the guardian of the rights and liberties of the people.

Madison changed his mind during the campaign in the cold winter of 1788–89 in part because he hoped that the addition of a bill of rights would satisfy a large number of people who had opposed ratification and reconcile them to the new government. Madison also changed his mind because Baptist ministers and lay leaders in his congressional district insisted on an amendment to the Constitution as soon as possible to guarantee the full religious liberty that they had been arguing for since well before independence, and that with the enactment of the Virginia Act for Establishing Religious Freedom in January 1786 they had at last won in part as a consequence of their petitioning campaign and Madison's labors as a member of the House of Delegates.

In the new and more democratic political culture that the American Revolution helped bring into being, large groups of people, like members of the Baptist church, could wield more political influence than ever before. Candidates like Madison had to pay attention to them and, if possible, make an agreement with them or, as Madison did, change their own minds. The 1789 congressional election in Madison's district furnishes one of the best early examples of how much had changed in Virginia since independence. Virginia Baptists rightly took credit for their role in using the changed conditions to persuade Madison to include the first version of what became the opening clause of the First Amendment in the Bill of Rights: "Congress shall make no law respecting an establishment of religion, or prohibiting the free exercise thereof."

Without the insistence of the Baptists in Madison's congressional district in 1789, it is possible that other men than he might have taken the lead in Congress in framing amendments to the Constitution. What might have been different? It is impossible to say with confidence, but it is possible that because Madison introduced his proposals early in the first session of the First Congress before anybody else did, his draft may have foreclosed other proposals for amendments that could have gone much further and could have altered the new Constitution more fundamentally as to structure and authority than the Bill of Rights ultimately did.

Madison angered some opponents of the Constitution whom he hoped to win over because the amendments that Congress submitted to the states in 1789 did not include any structural changes of the sort that men like George Mason, Patrick Henry, Richard Henry Lee, and William Grayson believed were essential. The Bill of Rights and the willingness of George Washington to serve two four-year terms as the first president and then voluntarily retire from office did, in the long run, contribute to the success of the new government.

30

Reasons of My Changing the Place of My Residence

EARLY IN 1798, the Norfolk printing house of Willett & O'Connor published a fourteen-page pamphlet written by David Barrow, a Baptist minister in Isle of Wight and Southampton Counties. Barrow entitled it *Circular Letter: Southampton County, Virginia, February 14, 1798*. A copy of the rare little pamphlet is in the Virginia Baptist Historical Society, at the University of Richmond, and the text is printed in Carlos R. Allen Jr., ed., "David Barrow's *Circular Letter* of 1798," *William and Mary Quarterly*, 3d ser., 20 (1963): 440–51.

The intended audience presumably included the members of the Baptist churches in which Barrow had preached for the past twenty years and other local residents of his acquaintance. The subject was his reason for leaving Virginia and moving to Kentucky.

The forty-four-year-old minister then had eight living children and owned and worked a small, unproductive farm. He had been the subject of mob action in 1778 when a group of Episcopalians seized him and another Baptist minister and dunked them in a muddy stream to mock their belief in adult baptism by immersion. By the 1790s, Barrow was a well-known and influential minister and had organized several churches in what in 1791 became the Portsmouth Baptist Association. Barrow believed that slavery was a violation of Christian beliefs and that it was also incompatible with representative government in the new nation, and he stuck to that position even though many of his fellow Baptists gradually abandoned their early opposition to slavery and, in many instances, became owners of enslaved people or beneficiaries of the slave system.

In 1785 and again in 1797 Barrow toured and preached in Kentucky. After his second trip, when the antislavery principles and actions of some of the Baptists he met there impressed him, Barrow decided to move to the west. Before he left Virginia, he wrote and published his *Circular Letter* to explain why he was leaving. The reasons he adduced were economic and had several causes, slavery being the root of most of them.

Barrow began, though, with four considerations that did not motivate him: "1st. It is not out of any personal prejudice against any man, woman, child, or party under Heaven." He clearly did not want it to appear that he disliked any of his neighbors or members of his congregations because they held different beliefs than he about religious matters or about slavery.

Second, "Nor is it to accumulate great stores of wealth for my children," and he quoted 1 Timothy 6:9, "For we are informed by the lip of inspiration, *That they who will be rich fall into temptation, and a snare, and into many foolish and hurtful lusts, which drown men in destruction and perdition.*"

Third, "Nor is it on account of the present deadness and coldness of religion; for I am well convinced in my own mind, that God will again revive his work in these parts." What Barrow meant was that he perceived during the 1790s that the energy and enthusiasm that had propelled the conversion of a great many Virginia members of the Church of England into the Baptist and Methodist churches had somewhat subsided.

And fourth, "Nor is it to get rid of temptations, trials and troubles; for we learn," from Job 5:6–7, "that *affliction cometh not forth of the dust, neither doth trouble spring out of the ground; yet man is born unto trouble, as the sparks fly upward.*"

Barrow then enumerated four "reasons of my changing the place of my residence." The first was, "I find by long experience, and constant efforts, that I cannot comfortably support my family, educate my children, and attend so much to public calls, as I have done, with my means, in this poor country, without falling into the line of speculation"—making investments—"or that of holding slaves, or sticking closely and personally to my farm. To let my family suffer is inconsistent with scripture and reason," for which he quoted 1 Timothy 5:8, "*If any provide not for his own, and especially for they of his own household, he has denied the faith, and is worse than an infidel.*"

Barrow elaborated on his explanation with, "The business of speculation, I think incompatible with the work of the ministry; or at any rate, it is very difficult duly to attend to both. And that of holding, tyrannizing over, and driving slaves, I view as contrary to the laws of God and nature. And if I must turn into the business of agriculture, which I think a safe and honorable employment, common sense dictates, that it would be most adviseable in a country, where the God of Nature has been the most liberal with his bounties, in respect to soil, &c." By the final decades of the eighteenth century in many regions of southeastern Virginia where Barrow lived and preached, the soil was exhausted, and even the most intensive cultivation often failed to produce profitable crops.

"Another reason," number two, "is, that by the sale of my property, I may draw enough out, to pay my just debts, which I have been obliged to contract for the support of my family, and other unavoidable expences, while I have been otherways employed: which I cannot do with my means, and comfortably subsist in this part of the union." That a minister who had several congregations to tend, sermons to prepare and deliver, marriages and funerals to conduct, and a large family to support should have debts and be in economic straits would have seemed a persuasive reason to Barrow's fellow Baptists and other farmers in his region, even those who did not agree with him about slavery.

Barrow then gave the third reason: "That I may, with the blessing of God, and common care and industry, be enabled to procure an honest, comfortable livelihood for my family, and be able, moderately, to educate my children."

And the fourth: "One distinguishing *trait* in the ministerial character is, *That he should be a man given to hospitality*. Whereas, in my situation, with my incomes, I cannot exercise that disposition as duty calls for, without severely feeling it afterwards; therefore, I leave this country, and move to one where nature has been more bountiful."

Moving for some or all of the reasons that Barrow adduced, hope for a better life in a new place, had been one of the most distinguishing features of the settlement and expansion of Virginia for almost two centuries by then. Barrow was one of many thousands of Virginians and other Americans who moved to the west during or after the American Revolution and created the new states of Kentucky, Tennessee, and Ohio, as well as other western states later.

Before Barrow left, he wished well to his fellow Virginians who remained in the state and expressed his hope that they would live well in peace and prosperity under the representative governments of the state and the nation. "I wish the total extermination of all errors whatsoever," including both political and religious errors, "and the universal spread and prevalence of light and truth.—The downfall of all despots and despotism; and that the *great trump of Jubilee may be shortly sounded from pole to pole;* that all the oppressed, in all countries, may enjoy the sweets of liberty, and *every man,* of all complexions, *return to his inheritance*—I wish that all Judges, and Courts of Justice, may be enabled to maintain integrity, and exercise impartiality!—I wish success to what *few honest Lawyers* we have!—But the downfall, or rather the speedy reformation, of all pettyfoggers, and knavish characters in this office.—And that all officers, whether civil or military, may not content themselves with empty titles, but hold and exercise their offices, to their own honor, and the good of the community."

Barrow then returned to and further explained his attitudes about slavery. "I wish that all masters, or owners of slaves, may consider how inconsistently they act, with a Republican Government, and whether in this particular, they are *doing, as they would others should do to them!*—" Barrow expressed sympathy for the plight of enslaved people. "I wish, most sincerely wish! That the poor, oppressed, naked, hunger bitten [*word torn*] may have patience and fortitude to bear up under, [*word torn*] honestly to do and perform their duty, (or rather wh[at i]s exacted of them) to their oppressors, and constantly pray, and look forward by faith, to that desirable time, when they will be delivered from the iron talons of their *task-masters,* and joyfully put off the galling yoke of slavery—" One more thing in that respect: "And by the way I wish, that all those who are so happy as to have been liberated, may behave themselves industriously, honestly and honorably to the cause of Liberty."

Barrow concluded his pamphlet with an expression of some of his deepest Christian ideals and with more quotations or paraphrases of biblical verses. "I wish Union, Happiness and Peace, to all married Pairs! and that they may *bring up their children in the nurture and admonition of the Lord.* That the uprising generation may excel their Fore-fathers in Knowledge, Arts and Virtue.—I wish success to all honest Merchants and Traders, by land and sea—I wish well to the Rich, and that they may *not trust in uncertain riches;*

but be charitable to the Needy, and use their treasure, *as good Stewards of the manifold Grace of God,* that those blessings may not prove a curse to them in the end." And, "I feel tenderly concerned for the Wicked in general, and most heartily pray! that all Lyars, perjured Persons, Drunkards, Thieves, profane Swearers, Gamblers, Knaves, Oppressors of the Poor, Whore-mongers, and Adulterers, &c. may speedily reform, and experience a sound conversion."

Thus, Baptist minister David Barrow in 1798 as he prepared to move from southeastern Virginia to eastern Kentucky, where until his death in November 1819 he was one of the most active Baptist clergymen and antislavery leaders in the state.

In the spring of 1815, Barrow wrote to Thomas Jefferson and apparently enclosed a copy of the minutes of a recent meeting of the Kentucky Abolition Society. Barrow expressed his admiration for Jefferson's political principles as well as his hope that religious animosities between differing denominations would vanish and not corrupt politics.

Jefferson replied politely at the beginning of May and repeated his often-expressed desire that slavery would eventually cease to exist; but by the nineteenth century, Jefferson had long since given up advocating the speedy end of slavery in the southern states. Jefferson also repeated to Barrow that ridding the country of slavery would require time and patience, and that as an old man, he had no expectation that he could take part in that work or that he would live long enough to see it through. Indeed, in spite of his repeated expressions of his dislike for slavery, Jefferson continued to profit from slavery and did exactly nothing toward ending it. He did not even publicly endorse the work of other people such as Barrow to end slavery or try to escape from its hold on him and the members of his family.

31

Death or Liberty, an Echo of the American Revolution

IN THE SUMMER OF 1800, an enslaved blacksmith named Gabriel and several other men in Richmond and in the counties of Henrico and Hanover organized the largest conspiracy in Virginia's history to overthrow slavery. Many old accounts of the event incorrectly give Gabriel the surname Prosser, but some of the contemporary trial records identified him as Prosser's Gabriel—his enslaver was Thomas Henry Prosser—to distinguish him from another conspirator named Gabriel who belonged to William Young. No records of the time suggest that Gabriel used his enslaver's surname. Many old accounts also characterize the event as Gabriel's Rebellion rather than as Gabriel's Conspiracy, which is the correct identification inasmuch as the conspirators never actually put their plans to rebel into operation.

According to the later testimony of one conspirator, the men intended to raise a flag above the Capitol that bore the words "Death or Liberty." Everybody knew the phrase "Liberty or Death," with which Patrick Henry had concluded his famous March 1775 speech in the Second Virginia Convention when he proposed to arm the militia to protect Virginians from the forces of their king. Twenty-five years later, and almost fifteen years before William Wirt published a biography of Patrick Henry that for the first time put a version of the speech into print, enslaved Virginians knew and clearly understood the irony that white men like Patrick Henry were willing to fight or die to preserve their own liberty but were unwilling to extend the blessings of liberty to enslaved people. The inverted phrase "Death or Liberty" expressed the firm resolution of the conspirators either to fight for their liberty or die in the attempt, or to threaten white people with death if they did not grant liberty to enslaved people.

A South West View of the Capitol in Richmond Virginia, Laurence Sully, engraving by Alexander Lawson and published in *Virginia & North Carolina Almanack* (Petersburg, 1802). (Library of Virginia)

The outline of the plan emerged during investigations and the trials of captured men who were suspected of taking part in the conspiracy. A party of about fifty men planned to rendezvous just outside Richmond during the night of August 30 and as a distraction set fires to buildings in the neighborhood known as the Brook. Then, the entire number of conspirators, which one participant estimated at a thousand, would slip into the city and take control of the Capitol and the penitentiary. They expected to seize arms stored at the two sites and even take the governor, James Monroe, prisoner or kill him. With the element of surprise and thus armed, the conspirators believed that they could bargain for their freedom or perhaps even for the abolition of slavery by stimulating other enslaved people to join their rebellion and by killing or threatening to kill the white people who stood in their way.

Unfortunately for the conspirators, at the appointed time and place of their planned rendezvous, a tremendous summer rainstorm washed out an essential bridge that they had to cross, which prevented them from acting; and then two men who planned to take part disclosed the plot to their enslavers. The governor immediately called out the militia and alerted the slave patrols to the impending danger. Within two weeks, the Henrico County commonwealth's attorney—the public prosecutor—had initiated the process of indicting and trying the men.

Trials of enslaved people accused of committing crimes—and insurrection, along with killing a white person, was the most serious of all crimes an enslaved person could commit—had taken place in Virginia since 1691 in what were called Courts of Oyer and Terminer, to hear and determine a case. Five justices of the peace served as judges and rendered their verdicts without the participation of a jury or legal process for a defendant to appeal a verdict based on an allegation of legal error in the trial. The law required a unanimous verdict of guilty to impose a sentence of death. The best that a convicted defendant could hope for in that case would be an appeal to the governor to commute the sentence to some less severe punishment or issue a pardon.

Between the middle of September and the beginning of December 1800, during the selection of presidential electors who in December would choose the president and vice president of the United States, seventy-two men stood trial in five jurisdictions for participation in the conspiracy. Courts found twenty-six of them guilty and hanged them, all but one of them in Richmond. Gabriel was hanged there on October 10. Even before Gabriel was captured and hanged, residents of the neighborhood in Richmond where the gallows stood asked that hangings be conducted elsewhere because the sight of frequent executions was too upsetting.

Governor Monroe informed Thomas Jefferson of what had taken place and that the government had "made a display of our force and measures of defence with a view to intimidate those people" who had not participated but might be sympathetic toward the conspirators. But, Monroe wrote, "Where to arrest"—stop—"the hand of the Executioner, is a question of great importance." Nobody felt safe with the idea that any of the conspirators could be allowed to remain alive in Virginia.

Jefferson replied that even in his own neighborhood, seventy-five miles from Richmond, where enslavers were perfectly aware of the need "for some severities" to keep the peace by terrorizing the enslaved population into not rebelling, "there is a strong sentiment that there has been hanging enough." In the midst of the presidential election in which he was a candidate, Jefferson explained, "the other states & the world at large will for ever condemn us if we indulge a principle of revenge, or go one step beyond absolute necessity." Jefferson suggested enactment of a law to provide for transporting some of the convicted men out of the state. That autumn, the governor asked for, and the assembly passed, a law to allow that form of punishment for convicted enslaved people who could not be safely allowed to remain alive in Virginia. Thereafter, sale of convicted enslaved people out of the state remained an option until the final abolition of slavery in 1865.

The phrase "Death or Liberty" on the conspirators' flag reminded everybody of the incompatibility of slavery and the principles of the new representative democracy that the American Revolution produced. Not long after the conspiracy, a visitor to Richmond recorded another echo of the American Revolution. He had heard a story for which there is no evidence for confirmation but that he believed was entirely plausible. At one of the trials, somebody told him, one of the conspirators had proclaimed, "in a manly tone of voice," "I have nothing more to offer than what General Washington would have had to offer, had he been taken by the British and put to trial by them. I have adventured my life in endeavouring to obtain the liberty of my countrymen, and am a willing sacrifice in their cause: and I beg, as a favour, that I may be immediately led to execution. I know that you have pre-determined to shed my blood, why then all this mockery of a trial?"

The phrase "Death or Liberty" and the comparison of the conspirator with George Washington leave no doubt that enslaved Virginians, as well as white Virginians, and presumably members of First Nations tribes in Virginia, all learned and remembered the legacy of the American Revolution and understood the promise of the Revolutionary language of liberty.

Gabriel's Conspiracy did not hasten the end of slavery or result in the freedom of any enslaved men other than the two men, Pharoah and Tom, whom the General Assembly freed for disclosing the plot before the conspiracy became a genuine rebellion. The conspiracy and the trials may have contributed to the reduction in white people's support for ending slavery or reducing its severity. That would be the most cruel irony of all, if an attempt to free enslaved people led to an increase in public support for slavery.

32

The Presidential Election of 1800–1801

THE FIGHTING OF THE War for Independence concluded in Virginia with the surrender of the British Army at Yorktown in October 1781, and the war legally terminated with the peace treaty in September 1783. Many Americans regard one or the other of those events as the end of the American Revolution. Some people suggest that ratification of the Constitution of the United States in June 1788 marked the end; or that the meeting of the First Congress and the inauguration of George Washington as president in April 1789 was the real end; or that ratification of the Bill of Rights in December 1791 should mark the end. I believe, however, that the conclusion of the unique presidential election that began in the second half of 1800 and concluded in February 1801 terminated the long series of legal and political changes—the revolution—that the struggle for independence and the Revolutionary language of liberty set in motion.

Why?

I have for many years, as here, made a distinction between the War for Independence and the American Revolution. It is true that the decisions that Congress took in 1776 on behalf of the thirteen colonies to exclude George III from their governments and to replace royal government with representative democracy—with republican government—were revolutionary acts. They were the beginning of a war and also of another series of revolutionary changes that played out differently in each of the thirteen new states. In some of the states, the decision to opt for home rule, for independence from Great Britain, set off struggles between or among groups of people to determine who should rule at home.

In Virginia, however, the elite political class that had ruled at the colonial, county, and parish levels for a century and a half retained its position of leadership. The traditional class of political leaders overwhelmingly supported independence by the summer of 1776. The Constitution of 1776 omitted or seriously weakened the institutions of government that royalty had imposed on Virginia or through which the king and his ministers influenced public policies in the colony, and it strengthened the institutions of government that Virginians had created and reinforced the ability of the tobacco planters and lawyers who had always been in charge to remain in charge.

The politics of fighting for independence and the experience of working under the authority of the new state constitution set loose other changes that had a revolutionary character but that, with one exception, just about nobody in Virginia desired or foresaw in 1776. That one change was also the most immediately important of them, the Act for Establishing Religious Freedom, which the Virginia General Assembly passed in January 1786 after almost two decades of agitation on the part of dissenters to enlarge the scope of religious liberty. The law abolished all of the privileges that the Church of England had enjoyed and all of the governmental authority that the church and its parish officials had exercised. The law converted all religious denominations in Virginia into voluntary, private associations.

That was definitely a revolutionary change in the government and led to even more revolutionary changes in the religious culture of Virginia. Within a few years, religious diversity expanded further and flourished. Congregation Beth Shalom formed in Richmond in 1789, one of the first six Jewish congregations in the United States; and Catholics established a missionary church in Alexandria in 1794 and not long afterward other churches in Richmond and Norfolk. Baptists, Methodists, Presbyterians, and other Protestant denominations thrived, too, in the new atmosphere of religious liberty.

In addition to the unprecedented petitioning campaign of Baptists that eventually persuaded a majority of legislators to pass the act of 1786, during the War for Independence, men in many Virginia counties complained to the General Assembly about terms of enlistment, exemption of overseers from conscription, the differences in pay between officers and men, and other military matters. They also filed complaints about tax rates, and some of them agitated for relaxation of the laws that governed slavery.

That, too, was something of a revolutionary change. During the colonial period people had merely petitioned for local or personal relief in the form of a law that affected only one person, one community, or a small group of people. Beginning early in the War for Independence, Virginians organized to petition the General Assembly on matters of important public policy. As a result, the old colonial politics of gentlemen standing for office and not being allowed to advocate or express opposition to any proposed changes to laws changed. Voters wanted to know what candidates for the General Assembly would do. Candidates, in turn, began to tell them.

Moreover, the innovation of recording the votes of legislators on important matters of public policy in the published legislative journals gave voters information of how candidates for reelection had already voted. By the time that James Madison got his nose frostbitten campaigning for a seat in the First Congress in the winter of 1788–89, electoral politics was visibly different than it had been only fifteen years earlier. It had become more democratic. The language of petitions and the language of public discourse also changed and became less deferential and polite, more honest and direct. That, too, was a significant change with democratic social implications of revolutionary importance.

The relaxation of the laws about the private manumission of enslaved people was of extraordinary revolutionary potential. For two decades, enslavers freed enslaved people, and their descendants remained free even after the antislavery impulse that the Revolutionary language of liberty generated in 1776 began to subside early in the nineteenth century. That the antislavery sentiment eventually dissipated almost entirely may have cast a shadow over the fact of the many manumissions and the consequences. Temporary though it was, the expansion of freedom, even if to only a small proportion of Virginians, was an event of great importance and potentially of revolutionary impact.

All of those events and others, when viewed in the long perspective of the historian, together constitute a revolution in society and government, a revolution that might not have happened had it not been for the necessity of declaring independence, explaining why, and fighting a war to secure it. Or those changes or other, similar, changes might have taken place in different ways or on different time scales, with differences in substance and in outcome impossible to predict. Those transformative events, all taken together, constitute the American Revolution in Virginia.

I believe that the concluding event of the fourth presidential election early in 1801 represents another landmark in the history of the American people that in several very important respects marks the end of the revolutionary changes of the era.

The election of 1800 was protracted even by the standards of the time. According to the new Constitution of the United States, members of an electoral college, not the voters, formally elected the president and vice president. In some states, the legislature chose presidential electors; in others and on different days and in different months, the voters elected them at large; and in still others, the voters elected them from districts, the same way as they elected legislators. Each state was entitled to two electors, as it was entitled to two senators, plus one for each of the representatives that it had in the House of Representatives.

The Constitution required that the electors meet in December and formally vote for president and vice president. Those electors met in their state capitals on the specified day and cast two votes. Then when the Congress opened and the president of the Senate—the vice president of the United States—counted the votes, the person who received the largest number was elected president, and the person who received the next largest number was elected vice president.

The men who wrote and voted to ratify the Constitution did not anticipate the evolution of the modern political party system. Indeed, they deplored any divisions within the political nation that pitted one group against another, which they condemned as factions, and which they believed were disruptive and dangerous to genuine liberty. They could not know in the 1780s that within a decade, differences of opinion about matters of national policy would create exactly just such divisions, and that as one of many consequences, people would begin to support two-member teams for national office, one a candidate for president and the other a candidate for vice president.

In 1800, President John Adams, of Massachusetts, was the preferred candidate of the faction that had come to be called Federalists, and a former minister to France, Charles Cotesworth Pinkney, of South Carolina, was the preferred candidate for vice president. People who had come to be called

Republicans, or Anti-Federalists, preferred Vice President Thomas Jefferson, of Virginia, for president, and former senator Aaron Burr, of New York, for vice president.

When the electoral college votes were opened and counted on February 11, 1801, Jefferson and Burr each had seventy-three votes, Adams had sixty-five, and Pinkney had sixty-four. The Constitution specified that in the event of a tie, the House of Representatives would elect the president, and in that election each state had one vote. The members of the House of Representatives from each state would have to vote among themselves to determine who their state would vote for or lose the state's vote entirely if they could not agree or were evenly divided.

And if that were not complicated enough, the men who had won election to the House of Representatives in the year of the presidential election were not scheduled to take office until December 1801. The congressmen, a majority of whom were Federalists, who were elected before the presidential election were the men who chose between Thomas Jefferson and Aaron Burr, the opponents of the Federalists.

The House of Representatives voted thirty-five times without making a choice. Eventually, probably from fear that the stalemate would paralyze the government and endanger the new system of representative democracy, or that some Federalist congressmen who personally detested Jefferson might elect Burr, several Federalist leaders persuaded a few Federalist members of the House of Representatives to allow Jefferson to be elected president. The vote was ten states to four, with the delegations from South Carolina and New Jersey divided and not counted.

On inauguration day, March 4, 1801, Thomas Jefferson took the oath of office as president, and Aaron Burr took the oath of office as vice president. Only one other time in the history of the United States has the choice of president gone to the floor of the House of Representatives, in 1825.

The most remarkable thing and the most revolutionary thing about the concluding event of the election of 1800–1801 was the action of President John Adams. Before daylight on March 4, Adams left town on a stagecoach to return to his home in Massachusetts. He did not remain to see his old revolutionary colleague and recent political rival succeed him as president. Many people regarded that action as undignified and insulting. Adams's departure from the new capital city of Washington was the revolutionary action that to my mind brought the epoch of the American Revolution to a close. For the first time in the nation or anywhere, a national leader peacefully yielded his office to a rival. John Adams, one of the most famous and influential founders of the nation, accepted his defeat at the hands of the people and went home to resume his life as a private citizen of the United States.

In the same manner that Patrick Henry and Benjamin Harrison had peacefully acquiesced in the will of the majority at the end of the 1788 Virginia Convention that ratified the Constitution of the United States that they had opposed, Adams quietly acquiesced in the result of the constitutional process that cost him his office, hurt his feelings deeply, and elevated his most talented adversary to the presidency. Adams did involuntarily what George Washington had done voluntarily, relinquish his office when his constitutional term expired. Adams did not publicly complain, he did not charge fraud, he did not claim a right to remain in power, he did not try to mobilize opposition to the new president, and he and his supporters did not threaten to secede from the new nation and form their own country. Adams's decision to accept the result of the election was bold, a decision that no prince, king, or emperor in the Old World had ever taken, nor could anybody imagine any prince, king, or emperor quietly yielding office to an adversary. Adams thereby cemented his place in American history as one of the greatest of the founders. He accepted the will of the people as expressed in the manner that the Constitution of the United States stipulated.

Thereafter, with only two exceptions in the next fifty-six presidential elections (in 1860 and 2020), the defeated candidates and their supporters peacefully acquiesced, however reluctantly, in the legal, official results of the election, of the legitimate process of the representative democracy that the heroes of the American Revolution created. Adams's early-morning departure from Washington, D.C., is what most people remember about him and about that day, but it was his acquiesence in the result of the election that was most important.

Thomas Jefferson also did something very important that day. It was, in fact, almost as important as Adams's decision. The new president delivered an inaugural address that, without intending to do so, explained the actions that Adams had taken and that brought the epoch of revolutionary change to a conclusion. After the bitter election campaign and the protracted voting in the House of Representatives that finally resulted in Jefferson being elected president, he reminded everybody that because the outcome had been "decided by the voice of the nation, announced according to the rules of the constitution," all Americans "will of course arrange themselves under the will of the law, and unite in common efforts for the common good."

Jefferson explained the essence of the new American representative democracy this way: "All too will bear in mind this sacred principle, that though the will of the majority is in all cases to prevail, that will, to be rightful, must be reasonable; that the minority possess their equal rights, which equal laws must protect, and to violate would be oppression. Let us then, fellow citizens, unite with one heart and one mind, let us restore to social intercourse that harmony and affection without which liberty, and even life itself, are but dreary things. And let us reflect that having banished from our land that religious intolerance under which mankind so long bled and suffered, we have yet gained little if we countenance a political intolerance, as despotic, as wicked, and capable of as bitter and bloody persecutions."

Jefferson continued by asserting his belief—and his hope that other Americans would also believe—that "every difference of opinion is not a difference of principle. We have called by different names brethren of the same principle. We are all republicans: we are all federalists. If there be any among us who would wish to dissolve this Union, or to change its republican form, let them stand undisturbed as monuments of the safety with which error of opinion may be tolerated, where reason is left free to combat it."

"I know indeed," Jefferson explained further, "that some honest men fear that a republican government cannot be strong; that this government is not strong enough. But would the honest patriot, in the full tide of successful experiment, abandon a government which has so far kept us free and firm, on the theoretic and visionary fear, that this government, the world's best hope, may, by possibility, want energy to preserve itself? I trust not. I believe this, on the contrary, the strongest government on earth. I believe it the only one, where every man, at the call of the law, would fly to the standard of the law, and would meet invasions of the public order as his own personal concern.—"

Jefferson concluded that section of his address, as we might expect from him, with a fine and elegant flourish. "Sometimes it is said that man cannot be trusted with the government of himself. Can he then be trusted with the government of others? Or have we found angels, in the form of kings, to govern him? Let history answer this question."

The history of the world and the history of the new United States provided a new answer. Elsewhere, kings and tyrants ruled the people; in the American states, the people ruled themselves according to the constitution and laws that the representatives that they chose had created. That was the true American Revolution.

A footnote: Soon after the election, Congress submitted and the states ratified the Twelfth Amendment to the Constitution. It empowered electors to vote separately for president and vice president, so that what happened in 1801 could not happen again. In the event of a tie or of no person receiving a majority, the House of Representatives, voting by state, would elect the president from among the three candidates who received the largest number of votes. If the electors failed to elect a vice president by majority vote, members of the Senate would elect the vice president from among the two candidates who received the most votes.

SUGGESTED READING

1. An Unconstitutional Act of Parliament

Greene, Jack P. *The Constitutional Origins of the American Revolution.* Cambridge: Cambridge University Press, 2010.

Kukla, Jon. "Grenville's Postponement of the Stamp Act Reconsidered." *Parliamentary History* 41 (2022): 406–25.

Morgan, Edmund Sears, and Helen M. Morgan. *The Stamp Act Crisis: Prologue to Revolution.* Chapel Hill: University of North Carolina Press, 1953. Has been reprinted several times.

Tarter, Brent. *Constitutional History of Virginia.* Athens: University of Georgia Press, Southern Legal Studies, 2023.

Tarter, Brent. *The Grandees of Government: The Origins and Persistence of Undemocratic Politics in Virginia.* Charlottesville: University of Virginia Press, 2013.

Tarter, Brent, and *Dictionary of Virginia Biography.* "Richard Bland (1710–1776)." Virginia Humanities online *Encyclopedia Virginia.*

2. What Is It We Are Contending Against?

Fichter, James Robert. *Tea: Consumption, Politics, and Revolution, 1773–1776.* Ithaca: Cornell University Press, 2023.

Hayes, Kevin J. *George Washington: A Life in Books.* New York: Oxford University Press, 2017.

Holton, Woody. *Forced Founders: Indians, Debtors, Slaves, and the Making of the American Revolution in Virginia.* Chapel Hill: University of North Carolina Press for the Institute of Early American History and Culture, 1999.

Ragsdale, Bruce A. *Washington at the Plow: The Founding Farmer and the Question of Slavery.* Cambridge: Harvard University Press, 2021.

Tate, Thad W. "The Coming of the Revolution in Virginia: Britain's Challenge to Virginia's Ruling Class, 1763–1776." *William and Mary Quarterly,* 3d ser., 19 (1962): 323–43.

3. The Alternative of Williamsburg

Ammerman, David. *In the Common Cause: American Response to the Coercive Acts of 1774*. Charlottesville: University Press of Virginia, 1974.

Fichter, James R. "Collecting Debts: Virginia Merchants, the Continental Association, and the Meetings of November 1774." *Virginia Magazine of History and Biography* 130 (2022): 173–217.

Fichter, James R. "The Mystery of the Alternative of Williams-Burg." Online *Journal of the American Revolution* (2019).

Holton, Woody. *Forced Founders: Indians, Debtors, Slaves, and the Making of the American Revolution in Virginia*. Chapel Hill: University of North Carolina Press for the Institute of Early American History and Culture, 1999.

4. The Yorktown Tea Party

Ammerman, David. *In the Common Cause: American Response to the Coercive Acts of 1774*. Charlottesville: University Press of Virginia, 1974.

Bowman, Larry. "The Virginia County Committees of Safety, 1774–1776." *Virginia Magazine of History and Biography* 79 (1971): 322–37.

Fichter, James Robert. *Tea: Consumption, Politics, and Revolution, 1773–1776*. Ithaca: Cornell University Press, 2023.

Rosenblatt, Samuel M. "Merchant-Planter Relations in the Tobacco Consignment Trade, John Norton and Robert Carter Nicholas." *Virginia Magazine of History and Biography* 72 (1964): 454–70.

Rosenblatt, Samuel M. "The Significance of Credit in the Tobacco Consignment Trade: A Study of John Norton & Sons, 1768–1775." *William and Mary Quarterly,* 3d ser., 19 (1962): 383–99.

Van Schreeven, William J., Robert L. Scribner, and Brent Tarter, eds. *Revolutionary Virginia, The Road to Independence: A Documentary Record,* 7 vols. Charlottesville: University Press of Virginia for the Virginia Independence Bicentennial Commission, 1973–83. Volumes 2–7 contain all of the surviving records of the county and city committees.

5. John Hook, of Bedford County

Bowman, Larry. "The Virginia County Committees of Safety, 1774–1776." *Virginia Magazine of History and Biography* 79 (1971): 322–37.

Fauntleroy, Juliet. "John Hook as a Loyalist." *Virginia Magazine of History and Biography* 33 (1925): 399–403.

Martin, Ann Smart. *Buying into the World of Goods: Early Consumers in Backcountry Virginia*. Baltimore: Johns Hopkins University Press, 2008.

Spence, Audrey K. "John Hook, Loyalist." *Virginia Magazine of History and Biography* 34 (1926): 149–50.

Tarter, Brent. "Introduction." Richard Slatten and Janice L. Abercrombie, eds. *Virginia Public Service Claims,* 3 vols. Athens, Ga.: Iberian, 1991–92.

6. Anthony Warwick, of Isle of Wight and Nansemond Counties

Bowman, Larry. "The Virginia County Committees of Safety, 1774–1776." *Virginia Magazine of History and Biography* 79 (1971): 322–37.

Fichter, James R. "Collecting Debts: Virginia Merchants, the Continental Association, and the Meetings of November 1774." *Virginia Magazine of History and Biography* 130 (2022): 173–217.

Fichter, James R. "The Mystery of the Alternative of Williams-Burg." Online *Journal of the American Revolution* (2019).

Van Schreeven, William J., Robert L. Scribner, and Brent Tarter, eds. *Revolutionary Virginia, The Road to Independence: A Documentary Record*, 7 vols. Charlottesville: University Press of Virginia for the Virginia Independence Bicentennial Commission, 1973–83. Contains scores of documents relating to county committees and loyalists.

7. College Camp

Berkin, Carol. *Revolutionary Mothers: Women in the Struggle for American Independence*. New York: Knopf, 2005.

Carp, E. Wayne. *To Starve the Army at Pleasure: Continental Army Administration and the American Political Culture, 1775–1783*. Chapel Hill: University of North Carolina Press, 1984.

Cox, Caroline. *A Proper Sense of Honor: Service and Sacrifice in George Washington's Army*. Chapel Hill: University of North Carolina Press, 2007.

Gillett, Mary C. *The Army Medical Department, 1775–1818*. Washington, D.C.: Center for Military History, United States Army, 1981.

Higginbotham, Don. *The War of American Independence: Military Attitudes, Policies, and Practices, 1763–1789*. New York: Macmillan, 1971.

Mayer, Holly A. *Belonging to the Army: Camp Followers and Community during the American Revolution*. Columbia: University of South Carolina Press, 1999.

Neimeyer, Charles Patrick. *America Goes to War: A Social History of the Continental Army*. New York: New York University Press, 1995.

Selby, John E. *The Revolution in Virginia, 1775–1783*. Williamsburg: Colonial Williamsburg Foundation, 1988.

8. The Battle of Great Bridge

Lawler, Andrew. *A Perfect Frenzy: A Royal Governor, His Black Allies, and the Crisis that Spurred the American Revolution*. New York: Atlantic Monthly Press, 2025.

[Scribner, Robert L.] "Editorial Note." William J. Van Schreeven, Robert L Scribner, and Brent Tarter, eds. *Revolutionary Virginia, The Road to Independence: A Documentary Record*, 7 vols. Charlottesville: University Press of Virginia for the Virginia Independence Bicentennial Commission, 1973–83, 5:8–10. Woodford's letter and reports are on 90–91, 98–103.

Selby, John E. *The Revolution in Virginia, 1775–1783*. Williamsburg: Colonial Williamsburg Foundation, 1988.

9. The Great Distress of Peter Anderson and Shadrack Furman

Frey, Sylvia R. "Between Slavery and Freedom: Virginia Blacks in the American Revolution." *Journal of Southern History* 49 (1983): 375–98.

Pybus, Cassandra. "Jefferson's Faulty Math: The Question of Slave Defections in the American Revolution." *William and Mary Quarterly*, 3d ser., 62 (2005): 243–64.

Selby, John E. *The Revolution in Virginia, 1775–1783*. Williamsburg: Colonial Williamsburg Foundation, 1988.

Taylor, Alan. *The Internal Enemy: Slavery and War in Virginia, 1772–1832*. New York: W. W. Norton and Co., 2013.

10. Mary Webley and Her Miserable Little Children

Bailey, Raymond C. *Popular Influence upon Public Policy: Petitioning in Eighteenth-Century Virginia*. Westport, Conn.: Greenwood Press, 1979.

Lawler, Andrew. *A Perfect Frenzy: A Royal Governor, His Black Allies, and the Crisis that Spurred the American Revolution*. New York: Atlantic Monthly Press, 2025.

Tarter, Brent. "'An Infant Borough Entirely Supported by Commerce': The Great Fire of 1776 and the Rebuilding of Norfolk." *Virginia Cavalcade* 28 (1978): 52–61.

Tarter, Brent, ed. *The Order Book and Related Papers of the Common Hall of the Borough of Norfolk, Virginia, 1736–1798*. Richmond: Virginia State Library, 1979. Introduction on 3–34.

11. No Inducement for a Poor Man to Fight

McDonnell, Michael A. *The Politics of War, Race, Class, and Conflict in Revolutionary Virginia*. Chapel Hill: University of North Carolina Press for the Omohundro Institute of Early American History and Culture, 2007.

Philyaw, L. Scott. "A Slave for Every Soldier: The Strange History of Virginia's Forgotten Recruitment Act of 1 January 1781." *Virginia Magazine of History and Biography* 109 (2001): 367–86.

Selby, John E. *The Revolution in Virginia*. Williamsburg: Colonial Williamsburg Foundation, 1988.

Tarter, Brent. *The Grandees of Government: The Origins and Persistence of Undemocratic Politics in Virginia*. Charlottesville: University of Virginia Press, 2013.

12. The Revolutionary Language of Liberty

Holton, Woody. *Unruly Americans and the Origins of the Constitution*. New York: Hill and Wang, 2007.

Howard, A. E. Dick. *Commentaries on the Constitution of Virginia*, 2 vols. Charlottesville: University Press of Virginia, 1974. Contains an extended treatment of the origins and evolution of the Virginia Declaration of Rights.

Tarter, Brent. *Constitutional History of Virginia*. Athens: University of Georgia Press, Southern Legal Studies, 2023.

Tarter, Brent. "The Virginia Declaration of Rights." Josephine F. Pacheco, ed., *To Secure the Blessings of Liberty: Rights in American History*. Fairfax, Va.: George Mason University Press, 1993, 37–54.

Tarter, Brent. "Virginians and the Bill of Rights." Jon Kukla, ed., *The Bill of Rights, A Lively Heritage*. Richmond: Virginia State Library, 1987, 3–18.

13. The Rising Sun of Religious Liberty

Buckley, Thomas E., SJ. *Church and State in Revolutionary Virginia, 1776–1787*. Charlottesville: University Press of Virginia, 1977.

Buckley, Thomas E., SJ. *Establishing Religious Freedom: Jefferson's Statute in Virginia*. Charlottesville: University of Virginia Press, 2013.

Isaac, Rhys. *The Transformation of Virginia, 1746–1790*. Chapel Hill: University of North Carolina Press for the Institute of Early American History and Culture, 1982.

Lindman, Janet Moore. *Bodies of Belief: Baptist Community in Early America*. Philadelphia: University of Pennsylvania Press, 2008.

Little, Lewis Peyton. *Imprisoned Preachers and Religious Liberty in Virginia*. Lynchburg: J. P. Bell, 1938.

Ragosta, John. *Wellspring of Liberty: How Virginia's Dissenters Helped Win the American Revolution and Secured Religious Liberty*. New York: Oxford University Press, 2010.

Spangler, Jewel L. *Virginians Reborn: Anglican Monopoly, Evangelical Dissent, and the Rise of Baptists in the Late Eighteenth Century*. Charlottesville: University of Virginia Press, 2008.

Tarter, Brent. *The Grandees of Government: The Origins and Persistence of Undemocratic Politics in Virginia*. Charlottesville: University of Virginia Press, 2013.

14. *The Patriots*

Baine, Rodney M. *Robert Munford, America's First Comic Dramatist*. Athens: University of Georgia Press, 1967.

Bowman, Larry. "The Virginia County Committees of Safety, 1774–1776." *Virginia Magazine of History and Biography* 79 (1971): 322–37.

Canby, Courtlandt. "Robert Munford's *The Patriots*." *William and Mary Quarterly*, 3d ser., 6 (1949): 437–503. Includes an informative introductory essay and the full text of the play.

Crawford, Meriah. "Robert Munford (d. 1783)." Virginia Humanities *Encyclopedia Virginia*.

Hubble, Jay B., and Douglass Adair. "Robert Munford's *The Candidates*." *William and Mary Quarterly*, 3d ser., 5 (1948): 217–57. Includes an informative introductory essay and the full text of the play.

McDonnell, Michael A. "A World Turned 'Topsy Turvy': Robert Munford, *The Patriots*, and the Crisis of the Revolution in Virginia." *William and Mary Quarterly*, 3d ser., 61 (2004): 235–70.

15. Should Will Be Freed and Emancipated from Slavery?

Schwartz, Marie Jenkins. *Ties That Bound: Founding First Ladies and Slaves* Chicago: University of Chicago Press, 2017.

Schwarz, Philip J. *Migrants Against Slavery: Virginians and the Nation.* Charlottesville: University Press of Virginia, 2001.

Tyler-McGraw, Marie. *An African Republic: Black and White Virginians in the Making of Liberia.* Chapel Hill: University of North Carolina Press, 2007.

Wiencek, Henry. *An Imperfect God: George Washington, His Slaves, and the Creation of America.* New York: Farrar, Straus, and Giroux, 2003. And *Master of the Mountain: Thomas Jefferson and His Slaves.* New York: Farrar, Straus, and Giroux, 2012. Controversial analyses of Washington and Jefferson and slavery.

Wolf, Eva Sheppard. *Race and Liberty in the New Nation: Emancipation in Virginia from the Revolution to Nat Turner's Rebellion.* Baton Rouge: Louisiana State University Press, 2006.

16. Hannah Lee Corbin (Hall), Housekeeper

Dawe, Louise Belote, and Sandra G. Treadway. "Hannah Lee Corbin: The Forgotten Lee." *Virginia Cavalcade* 29 (1979): 70–77.

Kierner, Cynthia A. "Hannah Lee Corbin (1728–1782)." Library of Virginia online *Dictionary of Virginia Biography.*

Kierner, Cynthia A. *Southern Women in Revolution, 1776–1800: Personal and Political Narratives.* Columbia: University of South Carolina Press, 1998.

Kierner, Cynthia A., Jennifer R. Loux, and Megan Taylor Shockley. *Virginia Women Through Four Centuries.* Richmond: Library of Virginia, 2013.

Tarter, Brent. *Constitutional History of Virginia.* Athens: University of Georgia Press, Southern Legal Studies, 2023.

Zagarri, Rosemarie. "The Rights of Man and Woman in Post-Revolutionary America." *William and Mary Quarterly,* 3d ser., 60 (1998): 200–227.

17. Lynch's Law

Evans, Emory G. "Trouble in the Backcountry: Disaffection in Southwest Virginia during the American Revolution." Ronald Hoffman et al., eds. *Uncivil War: The Southern Backcountry during the American Revolution.* Charlottesville: University Press of Virginia for the United States Capitol Historical Society, 1985, 179–212.

Hall, Randall L. *Mountains on the Market: Industry, the Environment, and the South.* Lexington: University Press of Kentucky, 2013.

Kegley, Mary B. "Fort Chiswell and Chiswell's Lead Mines of Wythe County, Virginia: A New Perspective." *Smithfield Review* 14 (2010): 52–68.

Tarter, Brent. "Lynch, Charles." John A. Garraty and Mark C. Carnes, eds. *American National Biography,* 20 vols. New York: Oxford University Press, 1999, 14:164–65. Contains citations to other accounts that purported to find the origin of the phrase "lynch law" in later events elsewhere.

Tillson, Albert H. *Gentry and Common Folk: Political Culture on a Virginia Frontier, 1740–1789.* Lexington: University Press of Kentucky, 1991.

18. Inferior Militia Officers

Buchanan, John. *The Road to Guilford Courthouse: The Revolution in the Carolinas.* New York: John Wiley and Sons, 1997.

Ethridge, Harrison M. "Governor Patrick Henry and the Reorganization of the Virginia Militia, 1784–1786." *Virginia Magazine of History and Biography* 85 (1977): 427–39.

Piecuch, Jim. *The Battle of Camden, A Documentary History.* Charleston, S.C.: Arcadia Publishing, 2006.

Russell, David Lee. *The American Revolution in the Southern Colonies.* Jefferson, N.C.: McFarland, 2000.

Selby, John E. *The Revolution in Virginia, 1775–1783.* Williamsburg: Colonial Williamsburg Foundation, 1988.

19. James, a Spy

Frey, Sylvia R. *Water from the Rock: Black Resistance in a Revolutionary Age.* Princeton: Princeton University Press, 1992.

Jackson, Luther Porter. *Virginia Negro Soldiers and Seamen in the Revolutionary War.* Norfolk: Guide Quality Press, 1944.

Quarles, Benjamin. *The Negro in the American Revolution.* Chapel Hill: University of North Carolina Press for the Institute of Early American History and Culture, 1961.

Salmon, John. "'A Mission of the most secret and important kind': James Lafayette and American Espionage in 1781." *Virginia Cavalcade* 31 (1981): 78–85.

Salmon, John, and *Dictionary of Virginia Biography.* "James Lafayette (1748–1830)." Virginia Humanities online *Encyclopedia Virginia.*

20. Continental Army Veterans

Appleby, Joyce Oldham. *Inheriting the Revolution: The First Generation of Americans.* Cambridge: Harvard University Press, 2000. Explores the experiences and attitudes of veterans through their published autobiographies.

McDonnell, Michael, and Briony Neilson. "Reclaiming a Revolutionary Past: War Veterans, Pensions, and the Struggles for Recognition." *Journal of the Early Republic* 39 (2019): 467–502.

Nudd, Jean. "Using Revolutionary War Pension Files to Find Family Information." Online *Prologue Magazine* 47 (Summer 2015).

Resch, John P. "Politics and Public Culture: The Revolutionary War Pension Act of 1818." *Journal of the Early Republic* 8 (1988): 139–58.

Royster, Charles. *Light-Horse Harry Lee and the Legacy of the American Revolution.* Baton Rouge: Louisiana State University Press, 1981.

Royster, Charles. *A Revolutionary People at War: The Continental Army and the American Character, 1775–1783*. Chapel Hill: University of North Carolina Press for the Institute of Early American History and Culture, 1979.

21. The Great Scarcity of Money

Garmon, Frank W., Jr. "Mapping Distress: Taxation and Insolvency in Virginia, 1782–1790." *Journal of the Early Republic* 40 (2022): 231–66. Documents widespread insolvency through local tax records.

Holton, Woody. *Unruly Americans and the Origins of the Constitution*. New York: Hill and Wang, 2007. Treats in detail the grievances of western men and women, including the problems of the shortage of cash.

Tarter, Brent. "Thomas Adams." John T. Kneebone et al., eds. *Dictionary of Virginia Biography*. Richmond: Library of Virginia, 1998–, 1:36–37.

22. The Inheritance of Catherine McCall

Crompton, Samuel Willard. "Randolph, John." John A. Garraty and Mark C. Carnes, eds. *American National Biography*, 24 vols. New York: Oxford University Press, 1999, 18:128–29.

Evans, Emory, and *Dictionary of Virginia Biography*. "William Byrd (1728–1777)." Virginia Humanities online *Encyclopedia Virginia*.

Ewing, Joseph S., ed. "The Correspondence of Archibald McCall and George McCall, 1777–1783." *Virginia Magazine of History and Biography* 73 (1965): 312–53, 425–54.

23. Live As If Free

Very little scholarship focuses on the subject of people whom enslavers allowed to live as if free, but some pertinent general studies of free Black Virginians are:

Boger, Tommy. *Free Blacks in Norfolk, Virginia, 1790–1860*. Charlottesville: University Press of Virginia, 1997.

Ely, Melvin Patrick. *Israel on the Appomattox: A Southern Experiment in Black Freedom from the 1790s through the Civil War*. New York: Knopf, 2004. Follows the experiences of the community of people Richard Randolph freed.

Gordon-Reed, Annette. *The Hemingses of Monticello: An American Family*. New York: W. W. Norton, 2008.

Mariner, Kirk. *Slave and Free on Virginia's Eastern Shore*. Onancock, Va.: Miona Publications, 2014.

McCleskey, Turk. *The Road to Black Ned's Forge: A Story of Race, Sex, and Trade on the Colonial American Frontier*. Charlottesville: University of Virginia Press, 2014.

Rothman, Joshua C. *Notorious in the Neighborhood: Sex and Families across the Color Line in Virginia, 1787–1861*. Chapel Hill: University of North Carolina Press, 2003.

Schwarz, Philip J. *Migrants against Slavery: Virginians and the Nation.* Charlottesville: University Press of Virginia, 2001.

Schwarz, Philip J. *Slave Laws in Virginia.* Athens: University of Georgia Press, Studies in the Legal History of the South, 1996.

Taylor, Alan. *The Internal Enemy: Slavery and War in Virginia, 1772–1832.* New York: W. W. Norton, 2013.

Wolf, Eva Sheppard. *Race and Liberty in the New Nation: Emancipation in Virginia from the Revolution to Nat Turner's Rebellion.* Baton Rouge: Louisiana State University Press, 2006.

24. Emigrating to Kentucky

Harrison, Lowell H. *Kentucky's Road to Statehood.* Lexington: University Press of Kentucky, 1992.

Sachs, Honor. *Home Rule: Households, Manhood, and National Expansion on the Eighteenth-Century Kentucky Frontier.* New Haven: Yale University Press, 2015.

Terry, Gail S. "Christian, Annie Henry." John T. Kneebone et al., eds. *Dictionary of Virginia Biography.* Richmond: Library of Virginia, 1998–, 2:223–24.

Terry, Gail S. "Christian, William." John T. Kneebone et al., eds. *Dictionary of Virginia Biography.* Richmond: Library of Virginia, 1998–, 2:234–35.

25. A Daring Attempt on a Very Important Part of Our Property

Schmidt, Fredrika Teute, and Barbara Ripel Wilhelm, eds. "Early Proslavery Petitions in Virginia." *William and Mary Quarterly,* 3d ser., 30 (1973): 133–46.

Wiencek, Henry. *An Imperfect God: George Washington, His Slaves, and the Creation of America.* New York: Farrar, Straus, and Giroux, 2003. And *Master of the Mountain: Thomas Jefferson and His Slaves.* New York: Farrar, Straus, and Giroux, 2012. Controversial analyses of Washington and Jefferson and slavery.

Wolf, Eva Sheppard. *Race and Liberty in the New Nation: Emancipation in Virginia from the Revolution to Nat Turner's Rebellion.* Baton Rouge: Louisiana State University Press, 2006.

26. Thomas Jefferson, Racist

Coates, Eyler Robert, ed. *The Jefferson-Hemings Myth: An American Tragedy.* Charlottesville: Jefferson Editions, 2001. Discounts the likelihood that Thomas Jefferson and Sally Hemings had children.

Gordon-Reed, Annette. *The Hemingses of Monticello: An American Family.* New York: W. W. Norton, 2008.

Gordon-Reed, Annette. *Thomas Jefferson and Sally Hemings: An American Controversy.* Charlottesville: University Press of Virginia, 1997. Made one of the first and strongest cases that Thomas Jefferson and Sally Hemings had children.

Jefferson, Thomas. *Notes on the State of Virginia*. William Peden, ed. Chapel Hill: University of North Carolina Press, 1955. The edition most scholars prefer and cite.

Miller, John Chester. *Wolf by the Ears: Thomas Jefferson and Slavery*. New York: Free Press, 1977.

Wiencek, Henry. *An Imperfect God: George Washington, His Slaves, and the Creation of America*. New York: Farrar, Straus, and Giroux, 2003. And *Master of the Mountain: Thomas Jefferson and His Slaves*. New York: Farrar, Straus, and Giroux, 2012. Controversial analyses of Washington and Jefferson and slavery.

Wolf, Eva Sheppard. *Race and Liberty in the New Nation: Emancipation in Virginia from the Revolution to Nat Turner's Rebellion*. Baton Rouge: Louisiana State University Press, 2006.

27. The Genius of Republican Government

Adams, Willi Paul. *The First American Constitutions: Republican Ideology and the Making of the State Constitutions in the Revolutionary Era*. Chapel Hill: University of North Carolina Press for the Institute of Early American History and Culture, 1980.

Tarter, Brent. *Constitutional History of Virginia*. Athens: University of Georgia Press, Southern Legal Studies, 2024.

Tarter, Brent, ed. *The Order Book and Related Papers of the Common Hall of the Borough of Norfolk, Virginia, 1736–1798*. Richmond: Virginia State Library, 1979.

Wood, Gordon S. *The Creation of the American Republic, 1776–1787*. Chapel Hill: University of North Carolina Press for the Institute of Early American History and Culture, 1969.

28. The Majority, the Minority, and the Constitution

Broadwater, Jeff. *George Mason, Forgotten Founder*. Chapel Hill: University of North Carolina Press, 1996.

Johnson, Claiborne F., Jr. "Federalists, Doubtful, and Antifederalists: A Note on the Virginia Convention of 1788." *Virginia Magazine of History and Biography* 96 (1988): 333–44.

Kaminski, John P., et al., eds. *The Documentary History of the Ratification of the Constitution: Ratification of the Constitution by the States, Virginia*, vols. 8–10. Madison: State Historical Society of Wisconsin, 1988–93. Includes all known surviving public and private Virginia documents and letters.

Ketcham, Ralph. *James Madison: A Biography*. New York: Macmillan, 1971. One of the best of the many biographies.

Kukla, Jon. *Patrick Henry, Champion of Liberty*. New York: Simon and Schuster, 2017.

Kukla, Jon. "A Spectrum of Sentiments: Virginia's Federalists, Antifederalists, and 'Federalists Who Are for Amendments,' 1787–1788." *Virginia Magazine of History and Biography* 96 (1988): 276–96.

Merritt, Eli. *Disunion Among Ourselves: The Perilous Politics of the American Revolution*. Columbia: University of Missouri Press, 2023. Thoroughly documents how each of the controversial differences of opinion among the states had arisen and grown before the Constitutional Convention.

Reardon, John J. *Edmund Randolph, A Biography*. New York: Macmillan, 1975.

Tarter, Brent. "George Mason and the Conservation of Liberty." *Virginia Magazine of History and Biography* 99 (1991): 279–304.

29. Baptists and the Bill of Rights

Berkin, Carol. *The Bill of Rights: The Fight to Secure America's Liberties.* New York: Simon and Schuster, 2015.

Buckley, Thomas E., SJ. *Church and State in Revolutionary Virginia, 1776–1787.* Charlottesville: University Press of Virginia, 1977.

Buckley, Thomas E., SJ. *Establishing Religious Freedom: Jefferson's Statute in Virginia.* Charlottesville: University of Virginia Press, 2013.

Ketcham, Ralph. *James Madison: A Biography.* New York: Macmillan, 1971. One of the best of the many biographies.

Labunski, Richard E. *James Madison and the Struggle for the Bill of Rights.* New York: Oxford University Press, 2006.

Tarter, Brent. *Gerrymanders: How Redistricting Has Protected Slavery, White Supremacy, and Partisan Minorities in Virginia.* Charlottesville: University of Virginia Press, 2019. On 14–16, discounts the likelihood that Patrick Henry gerrymandered the congressional district boundaries to place Madison and Monroe in the same district with the objective of keeping Madison out of the House of Representatives.

Tarter, Brent. "Virginians and the Bill of Rights." *Virginia Cavalcade* 32 (1982): 62–75. Reprinted with eleven other articles on the Bill of Rights from the *Virginia Cavalcade* series in Jon Kukla, ed. *The Bill of Rights, A Lively Heritage.* Richmond: Virginia State Library and Archives, 1987, 1–15.

30. Reasons of My Changing the Place of My Residence

Allen, Carlos R., Jr., ed. "David Barrow's *Circular Letter* of 1798." *William and Mary Quarterly,* 3d ser., 20 (1963): 440–51.

Lindman, Janet Moore. *Bodies of Belief: Baptist Community in Early America.* Philadelphia: University of Pennsylvania Press, 2008.

Miller, John Chester. *Wolf by the Ears: Thomas Jefferson and Slavery.* New York: Free Press, 1977.

Sachs, Honor. *Home Rule: Households, Manhood, and National Expansion on the Eighteenth-Century Kentucky Frontier.* New Haven: Yale University Press, 2015.

Sandlund, Vivien. "'A Devilish and Unnatural Usurpation': Baptist Evangelical Ministers and Antislavery in the Early Nineteenth Century, A Study of the Ideas and Activism of David Barrow." *American Baptist Quarterly* 13 (1994): 262–77.

Stanton, Lucia. *"Those Who Labor for My Happiness": Slavery at Thomas Jefferson's Monticello.* Charlottesville: University of Virginia Press, 2012.

Teute, Fredrika J. "Barrow, David." John T. Kneebone et al., eds. *Dictionary of Virginia Biography.* Richmond: Library of Virginia, 1998–. 1:371–72.

Traylor, Richard C. *Born in Water and Spirit: The Baptist Impulse in Kentucky, 1776–1860.* Knoxville: University of Tennessee Press, 2015.

Wiencek, Henry. *Master of the Mountain: Thomas Jefferson and His Slaves.* New York: Farrar, Straus, and Giroux, 2012. Controversial analysis of Jefferson and slavery.

Wolf, Eva Sheppard. *Race and Liberty in the New Nation: Emancipation in Virginia from the Revolution to Nat Turner's Rebellion.* Baton Rouge: Louisiana State University Press, 2006.

31. Death or Liberty, an Echo of the American Revolution

Nicholls, Michael L. "Gabriel's Conspiracy (1800)." Virginia Humanities online *Encyclopedia Virginia.*

Nicholls, Michael. L. *Whispers of Rebellion: Narrating Gabriel's Conspiracy.* Charlottesville: University of Virginia Press, 2012. Refines and modifies James Sidbury. *Plowshares into Swords: Race, Rebellion, and Identity in Gabriel's Virginia, 1730–1810.* New York: Cambridge University Press, 1977, and Douglas R. Egerton. *Gabriel's Rebellion: The Virginia Slave Conspiracies of 1800 and 1802.* Chapel Hill: University of North Carolina Press, 1993.

Schwarz, Philip J. *Twice Condemned: Slaves and the Criminal Laws of Virginia, 1705–1865.* Baton Rouge: Louisiana State University Press, 1988.

Wolf, Eva Sheppard. *Race and Liberty in the New Nation: Emancipation in Virginia from the Revolution to Nat Turner's Rebellion.* Baton Rouge: Louisiana State University Press, 2006.

32. The Presidential Election of 1800–1801

Inaugural address in Julian P. Boyd et al., eds. *The Papers of Thomas Jefferson.* Princeton: Princeon University Press, 1952–, 33:148–52.

Dunn, Susan. *Jefferson's Second Revolution: The Election Crisis of 1800 and the Triumph of Republicanism.* New York: Houghton Mifflin, 2004.

Ferling, John. *Adams vs. Jefferson: The Tumultuous Election of 1800.* New York: Oxford University Press, 2004.

Horn, James P. P., Jan Ellen Lewis, and Peter S. Onuf. *The Revolution of 1800: Democracy, Race, and the New Republic.* Charlottesville: University of Virginia Press, 2002.

Sharp, James Roger. *The Deadlocked Election of 1800: Jefferson, Burr, and the Union in the Balance.* Lawrence: University of Kansas Press, 2010.

INDEX